Secrets to Successful Families

Healing the Effects of the Past for a Better Family Life

Afshan Khan

Ta-Ha Publishers Ltd

First Published in June 2023

Published by: **Ta-Ha Publishers Ltd,**
Unit 4, The Windsor Centre,
Windsor Grove, London, SE27 9NT
United Kingdom

www.**tahapublishers.com**
support@tahapublishers.com

Written by: **Afshan Khan**
General Editor: **Dr Abia Afsar-Siddiqui**
Cover and Book Design by: **Shakir Abdulcadir**

A catalogue record of this book is available from the British Library
ISBN: 978 1 915357 10 6 (paperback) · 978 1 915357 11 3 (eBook)

Printed and bound by: IMAK Ofset, Türkiye
10 9 8 7 6 5 4 3 2 1

IMPORTANT DISCLAIMER: Any theories or statistics mentioned are included for reference only and are not intended to form any diagnosis. This book was written to share the real-life experiences of my clients, in situations that commonly occur, and which may be experienced by others. Names have been changed to protect the identities of the clients. This book is not intended as a substitute for the medical advice of physicians. The reader should regularly consult a suitable healthcare professional in matters relating to their health, and particularly with respect to any symptoms that may require diagnosis or medical attention.

Acknowledgements

In the name of Allah. We praise Him, seek His help and ask for His forgiveness. Whoever Allah guides none can misguide, and whoever He allows to fall astray, none can guide them aright. We bear witness that there is none worthy of worship but Allah Alone, and we bear witness that Muhammad is His slave-servant and the seal of His Messengers.

I dedicate this book to:

My mother, Shahnaz Naeem, from whose experiences, wisdom and teachings, I have greatly benefited. She provided a solid foundation for her children and built our ethos on sincerity, honesty, truthfulness and justice.

My father, Syed Mohammad Naeem, may Allah have mercy on him, whom I honour, respect and look up to in many ways. The struggles and hardships that he went through for his family have helped us all get where we are today.

My husband Mujtaba Khan; my children Asim Khan, Ahmed Khan, Ursala Zainab Khan and daughters-in-law, Sobia Khan, Nazia Khan and beautiful grandchildren Eesa, Rumaysa, Safiyyah, Aasiya, Juwairiya and Habeeba. I am grateful for their continued support and belief in me.

I would like to extend my gratitude and appreciation to Gülüzar Bayhan. She has been a great support, driving force and helper in this project. She has contributed through her writing and research in the sciences as well as ideas and thoughts.

And of His signs is that
He created for you from yourselves
mates that you may find tranquillity
in them; and He placed between you
affection and mercy.
Indeed in that are signs for a people
who give thought.

(Surah ar-Rum 30:20)

Contents

بسم الله الرحمن الرحيم

Introduction

Many common issues keep raising their ugly heads within our community and I have been compelled to write this series of books in a bid to enable us to move forward and overcome the common pitfalls that can needlessly destroy marriages and families. With Allah's permission, the first book, **Secrets to Successful Marriage**, has provided validation as well as practical solutions for many husbands and wives, as has the second book, **Secrets to Surviving In-Laws**, which deals with the much neglected issue of in-law relationships. This third book, **Secrets to Successful Families**, covers more complex marital and family issues in detail. Most of the common sources of tension and attitudes in marriage have a back story and root cause. This book addresses the common issues in marriages and digs deeper to find those root causes in order to effect lasting solutions. There are six chapters:

What is Behind Troubled Marriages? introduces the idea of emotional baggage that we bring into our married life and how this is at the root of our conflicts within it.

What Gives Rise to Emotional Baggage? delves into the idea of core beliefs and how certain core beliefs arise from specific childhood traumas.

How Does This Impact Married Life? addresses how these childhood experiences manifest as a range of issues in married life including lack of empathy, narcissism, and domestic abuse.

Self-Esteem is at the heart of the whole matter of family – the family we originated from, the family we have created through marriage and the way in which we parent our children and how they will go on to be as spouses and parents. Our behaviour stems from our self-esteem levels and this chapter details how to achieve healthy self-esteem.

Breaking the Cycle offers detailed marital and parenting advice to break the generational patterns that have embedded themselves in our psyche and are affecting our family lives.

Healing the Inner Child presents a range of practical personal growth tools from setting intentions and goals to du'a so that we can begin to heal ourselves as a basis for a stronger family.

As in the previous books, I will tackle the core issues head on, with the aid of real-life case studies, and provide solutions that have been tried, tested and successful in the light of my thirty-five years of counselling Muslim women, couples and young people. As an Islamic counsellor, it is not my job to issue *fatwas* (rulings) or to advise on the matters of *fiqh* (jurisprudence). However, through speaking with scholars and people of knowledge, and also my own study of Islam, I do include some basic Islamic advice. All Qur'anic translations in this book are taken from Abdalhaqq and Aisha Bewley's translation - *The Noble Qur'an: A New Rendering of its Meaning in English*.

We know that, ultimately, everything is in Allah's hand and only comes about by His permission. So if I had to give just one piece of advice, it would be this: when you are in the middle of a highly charged, emotional situation, think of what will please Allah – your Creator, and then the people. Doing just that will accomplish much. I pray that what you read in the coming pages will be of benefit to you and that Allah accepts it from me.

Chapter 1

What is Behind Troubled Marriages?

In the face of a troubled marriage, most spouses will blame finances, beauty, time spent together or apart, in-laws, parenting, growing in different directions and so on. Usually they are right. These factors play an immense role in the success of a marriage. However, these are all secondary reasons that conceal the deep-rooted and most common underlying problem – the **past**. In my thirty-five years of marriage counselling experience, marital struggles (whether they be temporary rough patches or longer periods of severe disturbance) are usually due to problems associated with a person's past.

Our past is a combination of our upbringing, our experiences, our relationship with our parents, siblings and wider society as we were growing up. Through these relationships we form **core beliefs** and worldviews that we carry through into adulthood. The person you are today is a result of everyone and everything that has been, which have cemented these core beliefs.

Our past shapes and defines our perception, our likes and dislikes, our fears and yearnings, our resentments and insecurities. It dictates the ease or difficulty with which we conduct a loving, respectful and caring relationship (not just marriage), and most importantly it defines our sense of self-worth in relationships. In turn, this determines our functionality as a human being.

Moving forward then, our marital relationships, parenting style, attachment and bonding all reflect our very own unique upbringing. Considering this, it is inevitable that any social pressures, financial difficulties, mental health issues, trauma, betrayal or loss that were experienced by our elder generations will have filtered down and fused into the genetic makeup of our own conduct, behaviour and perception. This is **emotional baggage**.

When we enter into a new chapter of life, such as marriage or parenting, this emotional baggage comes with us and affects our ability to perform our role as a spouse or parent. So in order to be the best spouse or parent we can be, it is important for us to understand the effect that our past has on us today and the effects it will have on our children going forward.

Alhamdulillah, we are in a financially, socially and emotionally secure position and have the opportunity, by the grace of Allah, to break the vicious cycle of emotional misbehaviour, break free from the shackles of ignorance and take the step to self-compassion, diligent and delicate self-care. In doing so, we will be doing a great service to our families, wider society and to our future generations.

So How Do We Understand Our Past?

We need to pull it out, put it on the table and actively process and digest it from an emotional, rational and spiritual perspective. Until and unless you go through this process, the past will keep raising its ugly head and sabotaging your every relationship and most destructively, your marriage. Once the past has been processed, the future can look a lot clearer, insha'Allah.

The first step in this process is to recognise that the 'enemy' is not the spouse and the 'problem' is not just current circumstances, but that heavy suitcase of emotional baggage that is the past. Consider that when two people bring their respective unresolved baggage to the marriage, allow it to fester for years and add to it, along the way, the stresses of social pressures and finances and in-laws and so on, it is not surprising that so many marriages are collapsing under the weight.

In the following chapters, I aim to highlight some of the common issues that people experience in their past, and the symptoms and manifestations of those issues in later life. I will guide you through how to actively process these issues with case studies as well as advice from the Qur'an and Sunnah. In doing so, together, we will break the cycle of unhealthy behaviour, embrace a positive and compassionate mindset for ourselves and others, and set the path for transformation; the transformation of us as individuals, of our relationship with our self, our parents, our spouse, our children and wider society for this *dunya* (world) and the hereafter, by the grace of Allah.

I appreciate that this journey will be long and difficult, as all transformative journeys are, but I passionately believe that it will be worth it. Before we begin, I would like to set out some pointers that will make the journey easier, insha'Allah.

Overcoming the Stigma

There is a false belief in the minds of many people that any mental health issues or emotional troubles are as a result of weak *iman* (faith), a poor connection with Allah or a lack of *sabr* and *shukr* (patience and gratitude). People who voice their issues or choose to visit a professional, such as a counsellor, are labelled as 'weird' or 'weak' in some way. Nothing could be further from the truth. Statements such as these can lead to the breakup of marriages, exacerbate mental health issues and cause deep personal distress.

In the same way that we make use of a combination of *du'a* (supplication) and advances in medical knowledge for our physical troubles, we must recognise that the same treatment method applies for our emotional and mental health concerns. We, as a community, must undergo an intellectual transformation and embrace mental health and emotional distress, be open to feelings and the process of healing in order to make way for a healthier society.

We must not labour under the misconception that the sufferers are few and hidden or that these issues will not touch us in our lives. This affects the women and men, elders and young people we have known for decades and have in our lives. They are us, we are them, and it is all of us.

The façade that we see in others and indeed the one that we put up ourselves, is only a veneer – an outer covering that we have built to protect the vulnerable, hurt little child inside that is holding onto the little things he or she still feels connected to in order to survive. The façade can be one of education, expensive clothing, high status jobs, lavish lifestyles but there is an inner child within each one of us that needs our attention.

Some of us are lucky enough to be able to attend to our inner child with time, self-reflection, pause, patience, and wider family support and understanding. Some of us will appreciate a helping objective hand and someone who can help us to look at it from different angles, such as a counsellor (individual or marriage counsellor) or therapist. There is absolutely no shame in this. In fact it takes a good deal of self-awareness and courage to recognise and reach out for the appropriate help.

Some people are afraid that they will not remain in control of the process if they see a therapist. I can assure you that you are in charge of who you let in, how far you want to let them in and the pace at which you progress. Others are not sure of how to reach out and begin to ask for help or they just don't know where to go, in which case an online search for Islamic counsellors may be a useful starting point.

When we remain inside our façades for too long, they can become prisons with iron bars of anxiety, lack of control, resentment, anger, depression and the list is endless. These issues eat away at us and then have damaging effects on our relationships with our loved ones and with Allah Himself. Once we lift our judgemental barriers about mental health and counselling or therapy, it becomes easier for ourselves and others to disentangle the issues that we may find ourselves caught up in. This is turn helps us to be better individuals as well as having a closer and more positive relationship with Allah, which is after all, the reason that we are on this earth.

Mercy

In a continuation of the above section about stigma, I would like to invite us all to extend mercy to ourselves and to our dear brothers and sisters and to be of those who make excuses for others. We do not know other people's pasts. We do not know their battles, fights and traumas, their daily struggles. We have no clue as to what made them the people they are today. This means that we must be gentle with everyone and have the most optimistic of thoughts about others – the people around us, the case studies mentioned in this book, to name a few. We need to have mercy with the creation, for Allah to have mercy with us.

Most importantly, we need to have mercy with ourselves. We

need to tell ourselves that it is okay. Perhaps you are the husband that has narcissistic traits, or you are the homemaker that has been abusive and severely angry with her husband and children, or you are the son that has been emotionally drained and occupied by your mother in her widowhood and are struggling to be a husband and father.

It is okay.

I mean it.

We all make mistakes. We all slip, trip and forget. Allah, the Most Wise, the Most Knowledgeable, knows what experience, what journey and what paths are best for us to cross in order to reach the best and most beautiful final destination.

Forgiveness

When we pull out the past and confront it directly, it becomes clear which issues are affecting us and how they may have come about. We may become more aware of how certain experiences have shaped us and how certain people have contributed to our core beliefs.

It is really important at this point not to hate or label or disconnect with the source of that emotional baggage; rather we must try to forgive in the process. A successful process will have, at its end stages, a development of empathy and understanding for those people in our past (for example, parents and siblings), who they are, how they came to be that way and embracing all of that as part of the journey that Allah wishes us to go through. We need to forgive the people in our past and extend our mercy to them.

This is not something that can happen in the initial stages of the healing process and it cannot be forced, otherwise it will simply lead to suppression and denial rather than an active processing of the past. But for the time being, we extend our mercy and make our excuses with the aim of forgiveness as a goal further down the line.

Hope

Ibn al-Qayyim explains to us that worship is like a bird; the head is love and the two wings are fear and hope. We cannot expect the bird to fly without the wing of hope. Given that we have the best of intentions, there is ease and beauty at the end of each trying, striving and working hard as the following ayah of the Qur'an states:

> ***Say: Allah rescues you from it, and from every plight...*** (Surah al-An'am 6:64)

It can be so easy to think that our efforts or the words of the counsellor are the key to the way out of our troubles. However, there is no success or removal of distress if this is not the will of Allah, the Most Merciful, the Most Wise.

This is where *tawakkul* (reliance and trust in Allah) is an important mindset to have. Developing the best of thoughts for and about Allah and only expecting greatness, blessings and beauty is a ground-breaking approach that we should try and adopt and implement, no matter how tough the situation.

> ***Allah is very gentle with his slaves.***
> (Surah ash-Shura 42:19)

There is no room for hopelessness even if there is sadness on the journey.

Next Steps

- Understand that current marital struggles are usually due to problems associated with our past and that our past has formed our core beliefs.
- Know that any emotional issues or difficulties that we have faced in the past and that remain unresolved show up as emotional baggage in our current relationships.
- Appreciate that a part of resolving current marital issues lies in resolving the past.
- Make the intention to actively resolve the past either by self-reflection or through Islamic counselling.

Chapter 2

What Gives Rise to Emotional Baggage?

In this chapter we will take a detailed look at some of the types of parental/carer behaviour and childhood experiences and scenarios that can give rise to emotional baggage. From this, we will be able see how core beliefs are formed and how they carry through into adult life even when those people and experiences are in the past.

By the end of this chapter, you should be able to identify your core beliefs and what has given rise to them and to be aware of how you are carrying these through into your present relationships.

The Past is the Seed of us Today

Parenting is like growing a seed. If we nurture it well, it will blossom and proliferate, not just for the lifetime of the children but for generations to come. Conversely, if the seed is neglected, then the ensuing damage and destruction similarly cascades through the generations. In this respect, parenting is an extremely powerful act and collectively has the ability to make or break a society.

For this reason, we have to tread carefully to see what exactly we are planting in the minds of our children – the husbands and wives of tomorrow that are the caretakers of the next generation. To put it bluntly, we are shaping the marriages and childhoods of the next few decades, while ours have been shaped by those who have parented before us.

This nurture sits in tandem with our nature – the bit of our personality that cannot be moulded and shaped but remains raw and natural. We have drives and wishes that reflect the deeper self and we can call this the **organismic self**, the most authentic and genuine form of oneself.

When our current self is far removed from our organismic self, there can be feelings of hopelessness and despair as we are always conflicted between the two. This is **inner conflict.** Often the turning point in someone's life comes when they realise that the person they have become is too far removed from the internal self that they were or would like to be. One of the consequences to this can be to lead a **double life.**

One of the most common comments in my practice is, "If you meet my spouse you would think they are charming and perfectly reasonable. You won't believe what I am telling you about them." Spouses are left wondering how their other half can be so supportive to others and yet so negative inside the home.

It is important to realise that most of us do have a separate persona for when we go outside. Just as we need to wear a coat to protect us from the elements, sometimes we wear a mask to face the world to hide the inner pain, imperfections and emotional baggage weighing down on us. At some point, we need to remove that mask, and that usually happens within the hidden walls of the home.

In addition to this, we can also struggle with the expectations of our community or wider society. Sadly, today's society puts great value on perfection and flawlessness – physically and internally. Even our experiences, lives and exposures have to be flawless and well-designed and this myth continues to be perpetuated through various media. We look at the perfect veneer that others present and this becomes a template for how we feel we need to live. It is a disastrous concept as it leads everyone to live several lives, which is exhausting. In the inner and intimate sanctum of a marriage, everything that was suppressed is now revealed. Sometimes it trickles out, and other times it explodes, but it always damages relationships.

The Role of the Family Setting

Although genetics plays a role in our ability to recover from traumas and self-regulate our emotions, I would like to focus on the role that the family setting plays – both the social environment in which we grew up, as well as the one in which we are currently living.

The family setting in which we were born and brought up has played a key role in shaping us as a child and also as the adult we have become. This, in turn, impacts our functionality within our current family setting which is our marriage and, thereafter, our capacity as a parent ourselves.

In order to improve the dynamics of our current family setting, it is therefore essential to take a detailed look back at our initial family setting as this is a key causal factor in the issues that we now experience. We have to pay attention to our upbringing and reflect on the single experiences and exposures that have shaped and designed our perception, understanding, fears, worries and the hidden concerns deeply engraved within us because they form our core beliefs. These then radiate back out through our behaviour in everyday life.

Core Beliefs

It is the core beliefs we hold within ourselves that shape the way we think about – and therefore act – in life, marriage, money, goals, ourselves and so on. Similarly, the core beliefs that our spouse holds will dictate to a great extent how they think and behave. This is why we may get frustrated with our partners and wonder how they could ever behave in the ways that they do, when in reality their thoughts and actions stem from their own core beliefs. It is their own 'realities' that have been shaped, moulded and put together through their experiences and every single breath since they were born. Reflecting on this and on the core beliefs of our loved ones and, of course, our own may help us to better relate, understand and explain behaviours, responses and perhaps certain reluctances.

Core beliefs are the ship we sail upon. In their entirety, they steer us in a direction. Sometimes, we are taken in directions by strong currents beneath us that we are not aware of. In the same way, some – perhaps even most – of the core beliefs we hold may be unspoken and unconscious even to our own selves. These aren't core beliefs that are uttered, revised and reviewed regularly. We have arrived at them through experience, exposure and perceptions and taken them to be our reality – and mistakenly – the only reality.

An initial step in identifying and becoming conscious of our core beliefs would be self-reflection and evaluation of our behaviours and thoughts. This is the starting point for changing those core beliefs that may be mistaken and thus those behaviours of ours that may be unhelpful or even downright damaging.

It is easier to explain the idea of a core belief by looking at case studies.[1] It becomes clearer to see how a core belief impacts a behaviour and contributes to emotional turbulence in a marriage.

1 These are all real life case studies that I have dealt with in my counselling sessions. However, the names have been changed to protect the identities of my clients.

Case Study: Finances meet Insecurity

His Background: Munir grew up in a family that was unstable socially and financially. There were always heated arguments about money, which Munir was exposed to. He heard comments implying that spending habits were linked to character and worth as a human being.

His Core Belief: Munir took on the idea that money equals happiness and security; that spending made you a bad person and that saving made you a good and sensible person, which determined your worth as a human being.

Her Background: Anila grew up in a household that exposed her to abusive words, threats and criticism. Her father always threatened to leave her mother and when she was 7 year old, he left the family home. Anila always felt guilty and blamed herself as the reason why her father left and ultimately why her parents separated.

Her Core Belief: Anila's core belief about herself became, "I am not good enough, I will never be good enough, and it's my fault that loved ones leave me." She was convinced that, "Anyone that loves me is likely to abandon me."

Emotional Turbulence: In the marriage, Anila spends money comfortably but Munir always feels she's overspending and calls her names that were learnt from his parents' arguments. He wants Anila to switch off the electricity and heating. This causes many arguments in the marriage and finally Anila starts to withdraw and constantly tells Munir, "I know you are going to leave me. Why don't you just walk out now?"

When it is laid out like this, it is easy to see how the couple react because of what they have brought into the marriage, which in turned has been shaped by the past.

Case Study: Responsible versus Irresponsible

His Background: Amr was brought up by parents who were very critical of him, constantly making unfavourable comparisons with others and repeating the idea that he would never succeed without their help. Whenever there is a problem in his life, they step in immediately and take over, even now.

His Core Belief: Amr has adopted the attitude that, "Whenever anything demanding happens in life, my parents will take care of it." He refuses ownership and responsibility for his actions and leaves his parents to deal with his issues. His core belief is, "I'm incapable of doing anything by myself, I just don't have the brain power" so he is unable to make decisions.

Her Background: Hafeeza grew up in a household in which she was the eldest of five siblings, with great responsibilities, ownership and a good sense of decision making. Her family, especially her parents, relied on her support, capability to lead and help with siblings and other duties regarding the day-to-day running of the house.

Her Core Beliefs: Hafeeza is a high achiever who is solution-focused and determined to steer her own path in life. Her core belief is, "If you want to get something done, do it yourself."

Emotional Turbulence: Whenever a problem arises within the marriage, Amr rushes back to his family, seeking help with the expectation that his parents will deal with the issue and find a solution. Hafeeza is constantly frustrated and very angry with her husband as she feels he is not stepping up and fulfilling his role as her husband. She criticises him for "not being a man." These clashing core beliefs as well as a lack of respect for each other are responsible for the marital issues.

Solution: In therapy we worked on Amr's core beliefs and changing his life lens from, "I'm dependent on my parents" to "I can do this myself." This required us to focus and disentangle his fear of failure which was the underlying reason for his reliance on his parents. With Hafeeza, we focused on communication techniques, incorporating patience, empathy and warmth, while steering her viewpoint of "being his mother" to "being a wife."

What you can do:

This is a good time to reflect on our own core beliefs. An easy starting point is to think about the last argument we had with our spouse:

- What was it about?
- What was my stubborn opinion?
- Why do I hold that opinion?
- What are the root causes or experiences that give rise to this opinion?
- What realities have I created in my head?

Have a think through these questions and some clarity might start to emerge.

Childhood Issues

There are an endless number of experiences in a childhood that can give rise to damaging behaviours and symptoms in later married life causing emotional turbulence. These range from those that occur in the family setting such as unintentional oversights in the lives of parents who already have their own battles to fight; others are external such as bullying at school or wars and migrations. Extended families, friends and increasingly social media, all play a part in shaping us. The following are just some of the main factors to consider when looking at what has formed our core beliefs, with real-life case studies to show the possible links between the past and the core beliefs that form and the marital issues these may give rise to.

Lack of Emotional Parenting including:

- Lack of affection and encouragement
- Lack of communication and respect
- Lack of time
- Passive parenting

In this case, parents make every effort to provide, in a practical way, the basic needs of a child such as food, clothing and schooling. There is no abuse in this scenario but there is also no positive interaction, meaningful communication or emotional nourishment provided to the child. In addition to having their basic physical needs met, children also need praise and positive attention, respect and engaging conversation.

Children, therefore, may develop insecure relationships with their parents because the latter were just emotionally unavailable, occupied or severely introverted. The child may have communicated their need but is simply met with parental unavailability. The result is that these children grow up feeling ignored and starved of love and affection, which may cause feelings of rejection and abandonment. This is not something to trivialise as it disturbs their sense of belonging, and makes them feel lonely and disconnected within their own family and home. The long term effect is a lower sense of self-worth, which can manifest itself as a needy, clingy, 'high maintenance' individual that constantly needs reassurance. This can be very tiring for the spouse as the following case study shows:

Case Study: Needs and Wants

Her Background: Jamila describes her childhood as hanging onto her elder sister's skirt. This is how she would view her mother: looking at her from behind her sister, wondering if she would get any acknowledgement. Her elder sister was her main carer while her mum was always too busy. She says, "Yes, my mother would cook, clean, look after our needs and shopping but all through my childhood I remember longing for a kiss, or a cuddle or some acknowledgement that I'm here, I'm worthy, I'm important to her, and that I matter."

Her Core Belief: Jamila recalls her childhood with sadness and sometimes still feels the heavy weight of that absence. She seeks that lack of attention from her husband and her core belief is to "expect the worst" in terms of being loved.

Emotional Turbulence: Hamad feels that Jamila is high maintenance, emotionally needy and constantly requiring reassurance. He is too tired to do this and this leaves Jamila feeling unimportant and leads to arguments.

Aggregive Parenting including:

- Interference and control
- Anger
- Criticism
- Favouritism

There are those parents who are highly achieving, have meticulous standards and exaggerated expectations of their children. They will 'hover' and swoop in to help their children too soon and too often, never allowing them to fail, fall or forget. They will micro manage every aspect of their child's life from what, when and how they should eat, dress, study and spend their leisure time and with whom. These children have no space to grow, think, feel or find their way. When, as inevitably they will, these children fail to live up to their parents' high expectations, they are subject to criticism and an angry response. Those comments are more than words; they stay with those children and affect them later in life in terms of their behaviour and responses.

While they may seem 'successful' in academic terms when they are younger, they may grow up to lack confidence, trust and awareness of their own capacity and abilities. They worry about failure and this limits what they are willing to try. They may never gain responsibility, ownership, independence and self-confidence as adults as they will be always looking for a safety net in their lives.

Case Study: Control Issues

Her Background: Tehmina was shouted at, belittled and controlled continually as a child by her over-achieving parents. No matter how hard she tried, her grades were never high enough, she was never slim enough, she was never talented enough.

Her Core Belief: In order to please everyone she developed the core belief that, "I have to change myself to please others. I must push myself to exceed."

Emotional Turbulence: As a young adult, she was constantly worried about what other people thought of her and how they saw her. This was consuming her thoughts to the point of being overwhelming and debilitating. She began overdoing things, going out of her way to please others in order to be loved and accepted, all the while losing her own sense of self. In the end, she developed bulimia due to feeling disgusted about herself and needing to have some control over some part of her life.

This case study shows that the devastating effects of such parenting cannot be underestimated. Linked to this type of critical parenting is the issue of **favouritism** that may sound trivial but that has disastrous consequences deep into adulthood.

Favouritism can be unconscious. Although the natural notion is that all parents love their children equally, it is also natural for a mother or father to sometimes be inclined towards one child slightly more due to their vulnerability, personality or simple similarity of wavelengths. However, this is not supposed to create a difference in the treatment of siblings by parents. While an adult has no control over their heart, even if there are certain differences in feelings, the children must never know, but that is not always the case in real life.

Unfortunately, this behaviour can also be conscious and some parents deliberately target one child in favour of another or even in favour of themselves. Think of a child who has constant comparisons made against them. He is the target of the family, the scapegoat, the black sheep. Nothing she ever does is good enough. These take the form of comments such as:

"Why can't you be more like your brother. He studies so hard."

"When I was your age, I walked 3 km to school and back and then helped my mother in the kitchen."

Such children grow up to either procrastinate as adults in their married life and never take responsibility because they have already learnt that they will fail; or they will become self-centred as they feel that now is their time to shine.

Case Study: Procrastination

His Background: Rayan was the eldest child in the family. He did not speak till late and was a rather sickly child. His younger brother, by two years, was brighter, smarter, more popular and better looking. Rayan's father would constantly compare Rayan to his younger brother, asking him why he couldn't be more like him. This started from when Rayan was 5 and went on until his father died, just before he got married. Rayan says, "I can hear his words before I start anything: that you are going to fail. He said it. I believed it. I made myself believe it. When my father was lying on his deathbed, I could not find it in my heart to forgive him. I could not go near him. It seemed as if there was a wall between us, that he had built up, that I feel has affected my life and ruined it in every way."

His Core Belief: Rayan is resigned that, "I will fail, so there is no point in trying. I will never succeed. My father died being disappointed in me."

Emotional Turbulence: Layla complained that Rayan was a procrastinator. Even though he had talents and was skilled, whenever he started a project, he would leave it because he had set himself up for failure. Layla said, "I am always there for him, I look after the children. However he is not involved, he cannot do anything by himself. He struggles. He does not need a wife he needs a mother." She was clearly frustrated.

Rayan had lost the trust and belief in himself which was debilitating. He was fixated and focused on the one thing that could possibly lead to failure. He accepted defeat and loss before there was any reason to do so, and felt no desire to fight against that and prove himself.

Excessive Responsibility

We find too many young girls who grow up taking responsibility for tasks that an adult should be doing – looking after mother, father, taking care of household chores, cooking, washing, parenting a sibling. She never receives positive verbal affirmation, appreciation, love, affection and protection as a child. She was never allowed to be young and carefree.

This role of hers that she has perfected – to people please, to be submissive, to shoulder enormous responsibilities – is now her comfort blanket to the extent that she cannot be or think in any other way. The danger is that she will grow up to be a co-dependent wife to a narcissistic husband who thrives on her submissiveness to bolster his own ego. Despite her getting divorced from her first husband who was narcissistic, she gets married again to a similar man. The narcissist/co-dependent relationship is explored further in the next chapter.

Similarly, there are too many boys that grow up always taking care of the entire family and even those who are 'back home'. Their entire childhood is shaped and filled with memories to do with providing and running after others' needs. Growing up they may get some satisfaction and ego boost by feeling they are capable, however their primary needs aren't met by any other individuals. They are in a position where they are giving all their time, which can lead them to become very depleted.

In their marriage, often their first intimate relationship, they find space and allow themselves to offload and express their anger, frustration and deep resentment to their wives. This may be not be apparent but suppressed anger from the past then becomes baggage that is carried into the marriage. Sometimes, people may not be conscious of their suppressed emotions and only come to realise when they are in the most intimate relationship and cannot hold on any longer to their masks and covers.

Alternatively, they may continue in their responsible mode and become controlling husbands because they do not know how else to be. They may entirely neglect their married families in favour of their parents and siblings.

Excessive responsibility may (but not always) arise on the death of a parent. A widowed parent may find themselves feeling overly possessive about their child and be threatened by their increasing independence or 'sharing' them with a spouse, which can lead to an additional layer of challenge for the spouse. This type of behaviour is **narcissistic parenting.**

Case Study: Replacement Father

His Background: Jamal's father passed away when he was 11 and being the eldest child he had to grow up very quickly and become the 'replacement father'. He helped his mother with the finances and married off his sisters.

His Core Belief: Jamal was determined that, "I must look after my mother and siblings at all cost. It is my sole responsibility."

Emotional Turbulence: After all his siblings got married off, he was able to marry in his 30s. He struggled and did not know how to balance being a son as well as a husband. His life was still bound to his mother and he was surrendering to her needs and those of his siblings, on the orders of his mother. Nabila found it difficult to cope with as she and her children were always placed second in her own husband's life.

Bullying

We may associate bullying with what happens in the school playground, but it can also happen within the home and, sadly, be perpetrated by members of the family. It may be because of a physical difference, such as weight, or an introverted personality, that sometimes family members pick on one of their own and make them the centre of jokes and ridicule. The truth is, it may start off as a light comment, but other extended family members – siblings, aunts, uncles, cousins – can jump on the bandwagon to deflect from their own issues or to cover their own insecurities. Make no mistake. This is bullying and can destroy a young person's self-belief.

Although this is family bullying, one cannot think it remains just under that roof and in that house. Due to damaged self-esteem, the child is scarred and vulnerable. They may become introverted or labelled 'weird'. Potential 'abusers' in school, for example, can take advantage of this and so what started as light bullying at home can spread across the spectrum to school and later the work place.

Abuse

Some adults are so scarred and so traumatised themselves as to project their anger and frustrations on their children or other young ones in their care. This can take the following forms:

- Sexual assault, rape, sexual violence
- Physical violence, domestic abuse
- Emotional and psychological abuse
- Neglect
- Harassment
- Injustice.

Child abuse is a stain upon humanity and sadly almost a taboo. It is heart-breaking to see, find out and face the realities that take place behind closed doors. Abuse has no colour, no shape nor does it have a certain socio-economic or psycho-social state. It takes place in the most hidden and most unexpected homes and rooms and no child ever deserves to be treated this way. But the reality is that children **are** treated like this and they become scarred adults on every level. This is not something that society at large can ignore and pretend is not happening.

Case Study: Vicious Cycle

His Background: Saeed was severely abused by his father. Over any small excuse, he would be regularly hit and beaten and even picked up and thrown across the room from one wall to the other.

His Core Belief: Unsurprisingly, Saeed's core belief was simply, "I am worthless. I do not deserve to exist."

Emotional Turbulence: Hana has been married to Saeed for 8 years and says that there hasn't been a week where he hasn't hit her or thrown something at her. He swears and shouts all the time. Hana is ready to leave. Saeed cannot get past his own childhood anger, rage and frustration and this is all pouring out on Hana.

Sexual Abuse

In some cultures, this is simply not spoken about or acknowledged and this adds an extra layer of guilt to the young person's trauma. It may be that parents are approachable but the norm is that sexual abuse is cloaked in shame and secrecy and almost all the people who come to my practice believe that this was in some way their fault. Just knowing and believing that sexual abuse is never the fault of the child can relieve a huge burden from the now adult victim's shoulders. In fact, in cases of sexual abuse the people who come to me are giving voice to their experiences for the first time. This is so important. If you cannot talk to anyone about your struggles and hardship, if you suffer in silence, then you are stuck in darkness and there is no clarity or chance to move on.

The story starts off the same: She comes to me in her 20s, 30s or even 40s. She says she feels lost, unable to look after the house and the children. Her anxiety levels are so high and the panic attacks so severe that she no longer leaves the house. She can no longer function normally. "What's wrong with me?" she asks me with tears in her eyes. This is the story of one woman[2] who experienced abuse within her own home, although the effects of abuse carried out in the institutions we are sent to as children are no less severe.

Case Study: Protection and Safety?

Her Background: "When I was a child, in primary school, perhaps around 5 years old, there was someone else who lived with us. He would secretly touch me, come very close to me and sometimes he would expose himself to me. This continued for 3 years. I did not know who to talk to. I became very sad, withdrawn and stopped interacting with others. After a while I'd get called names and told I was weird because I couldn't make any friends anymore. Life wasn't good at home or at school. I couldn't tell anyone. He left after 3 years and I tried to convince myself that it was in the past."

Her Core Belief: Samina deeply internalised the idea that she was shameful, dirty, worthless and that, "There is something wrong with me."

2 This is not to deny that boys can be and are victims of sexual abuse.

Emotional Turbulence: Fifteen years later, Samina got married, and it was then that she had her first severe panic attack. It didn't take her long to realise she was always in a state of high anxiety and unable to function normally in daily life and within the marital relationship.

A child subject to sexual abuse is constantly vigilant about how someone will approach them, constantly in fear of being violated, all the while carrying feelings of guilt and shame about their own body. Who can they trust? Who can they tell? This carries through life as severe anxiety, depression and even physical illness.

***

In my years of experience, these are the general patterns that seem to have emerged between past background, formation of core beliefs and current marital issues. None of the above core beliefs, I am suggesting are definitely caused by the examples I have provided. I have simply shared my experience. The causes and underlying reasons may be completely different and it is always interesting to explore other contributory factors. When it comes to psychology, human behaviour and learning, it is hard to point at one thing and assume there is a causal relationship.

It may be the case that some of these issues did not affect you directly as a child, but affected your parents, and the traumas and learned behaviours have passed down the generations. There are as many parenting styles as there are parents and the unique nature and genetic predisposition of every child and their singular experiences all make for a distinctive adult personality. This is what makes counselling such a rich experience. There are no pre determined solutions to a particular problem.

We will all have experienced something that shapes the way we function as a spouse and parent ourselves, as the saying goes, "No one escapes childhood unscathed."

The point of this chapter is not to criticise our parents or harbour any resentment towards them. Duty to our parents stems from piety and I emphasise the importance of our parents and our care towards them in Islam.

Our parents may have been through wars, migrations, political unrest, estrangement from their parents, suffered racism and poverty at closer quarters than we ever may. Those kind of experiences at that level can make someone bitter, cynical, hopeless and full of hatred and anger. They may not have had the support, space or resources to work through their accumulated distress and frustration and so this may have spilled out onto their spouses and children. These are the forces that also shape us.

I have had clients say to me:

"I want to have a relationship with my mother. I always wanted to be like others and be able to tell them how close I am with my mother and all the lovely things we do, but I have nothing that I can share, nothing except all the awfulness my mother releases onto me and has done since I was a kid."

"My father was always critical, used swear words, and never showed me any affection, I don't know what it means to have a father."

The purpose of this chapter is for us to embrace our own feelings and emotions, accept them and to learn how to manage them in a way that doesn't perpetuate the cycle. It is about working towards forgiveness, developing an insight into why our parents became the parents they were, or are, with compassion and understanding. It doesn't mean distancing from our parents, but it also does not mean that we leave ourselves open to receive destructive behaviours from them that affect us and future generations adversely.

For a generation to break the cycle of trauma is not an easy task. It requires personal strength, great levels of patience and a solid sense of self-esteem. For this, I strongly advise my readers to build up their emotional resistance and acquire the resilience they need to thrive in their circumstances, either through self-work or with professional help.[3] Throughout the book, I have highlighted ways in which to do this, but a good starting point is to think of these behaviours as an illness. Just knowing that it is not personal can often bring a little calm.

Next Steps

- Explore what your core beliefs might be using the exercise on page 24
- Reflect on how close you feel to your authentic self. Do you feel conflicted inside? Do you feel that you lead a double life?
- Out of 10, what would you say is the level of emotional turbulence in your marriage?

3 Professional help can be useful when more support and guidance is needed and is absolutely essential in more serious cases, where, for example, any type of abuse has happened or when self-work has reached a plateau.

Chapter 3

How Does This Impact Married Life?

In the previous chapter, we focused on a variety of scars that we may have got from our childhood, teens or perhaps later. These experiences don't let us go nor do they leave us. Childhood stress doesn't magically disappear. Traumas are an imprint that don't just dissolve into thin air. Pretending they didn't happen or avoiding dealing with them is unhelpful in the long run. In fact, this may even cause greater and deeper issues in later years.

This is the emotional baggage that often comes to the surface after marriage. It can be covered up for a few years, perhaps even decades, but all it takes is one little trigger, one seemingly unrelated incident that can lead to a brutal breakdown or explosion that can resemble the very same incident that caused and created the trauma to begin with. Even when that happens, my clients may walk into my room saying, "I don't know why I feel like this, I don't know what's wrong with me." For all those that say, "I've got over my childhood, I have dealt with it", "I'm fine now", I would ask you to keep reading.

Nothing Leaves You

His legs are shaking, her voice is getting quieter, their pupils are dilating. The body language of my clients, their voices, their eyes, their hands, their posture all tell me something. While they are saying, "I'm fine now", "Things haven't really affected me that much", "It's all over now", their body is silently screaming, "That's not true!!" It is true that the causes may no longer be present, existent or perhaps influential. Circumstances change, environments change, our adaptation and dealing mechanisms change and become more advanced in some cases. However, the 'effects' on you are still there, like the brown water mark that is left on the page long after the water has dried.

Because the effects are within you, they deepen and become part of your fabric without effort. They are an inseparable aspect of your personality and life. The fact is that the unconscious mind will react in a certain way in response to all that it was subject to. Your body and heart may not like it or choose it. However, your unconscious mind will have absorbed everything. It saw it, accepted and embraced it, and through constant replaying and perhaps in a complex way, it chooses to always gravitate towards it and this will manifest as symptoms.

Not all of these symptoms are due to emotional issues. Sometimes you can be run down, have suffered a recent bereavement, or just not taken care of yourself. However, for the purposes of this book, these are the symptoms that I feel, in my experience, may be the overspill of a 'past story' into the present psyche.

Commonly, most people struggle with trying to please everyone, sort out the house chores, manage the parenting, be a spouse, look after other members of the family. This can lead to anger and frustration that becomes increasingly harder to contain and is now being released on other family members.

Then there is the person who is desperately trying not to be like the parent they had: the angry mother or the unemotional father, but this is not as easy as they had imagined. Because, of course, the forces that shaped their parent into anger or unavailability haven't just disappeared. So the adult child watches helplessly as they perpetuate the cycle of anger, resentment and frustration for their own children, when they swore that they wouldn't be like that.

More seriously, unresolved emotional issues can manifest as mental health conditions such as anxiety disorders, depression, bipolar, and in particular, personality disorders. Examples of the latter are borderline personality disorder, narcissistic personality disorder or emotional instabilities and these can often be misinterpreted and left undiagnosed for many decades.

Past traumatic experiences can lead to low moods, deep sadness, hopelessness, changes in personality traits and formation of imbalanced core beliefs that perpetuate negative thinking and behaviour. At more extreme levels, there may be issues with addiction, domestic violence and suicide ideation.

There are, of course, a host of factors that contribute to mental health disorders. In some people, research has shown that, for instance, generalised anxiety disorder can appear after the age of 35 without any particular traumatic events or experiences happening in the life of the sufferer.

In this chapter, I will address the topic of mental health and in particular some of the mental health illnesses that I see regularly in my counselling sessions, how they relate to the emotional baggage that is unpacked and the patterns that I see emerging. Nevertheless, I must again emphasise that every case of mental health illness is unique and needs to be dealt with, with great care.

Most of the issues that I see in my practice can come under the following headings and we will look through these in detail:

- Low self-esteem
- Lack of emotion/stonewalling
- Intimacy issues
- Anxiety/depression
- Anger
- Infidelity to a lesser or greater degree
- Narcissist/co-dependent dynamic
- Domestic violence and abuse
- Addiction
- Pornography
- Suicide ideation.

These issues do not arise in a marriage out of nowhere and often multiple of these issues will show up or increase in intensity over time. The starting point for resolving the issue may not be the marriage itself but what each person has brought into the marriage and that means going back into the past. As a child you carry the past with you like a comfort blanket and as an adult, it becomes part of you and you do not stop carrying it. It is still with you when you are in your marriage and when you have children. Before I deal with these issues, I would like to take a brief look at the rationale behind the people we choose to marry because that can also be quite revealing.

Who Do We Marry?
How Do We Get Ourselves Into This?

Our past doesn't just affect our behaviour within marriage, it may also influence WHO we marry in the first place. In my practice, I see a pattern in the spouses that people choose for themselves and in a significant proportion of couples, people choose spouses similar to their own parents, albeit subconsciously.

It is interesting to see their reaction when they realise this too and say, "Oh my goodness, I married someone just like my mum!", or "That's just like my dad." By that I do not mean in physical terms but there is an attraction to a behaviour or thought process that makes people gravitate to a spouse similar to their parents. There is the danger then, of the patterns of the past being repeated and imbalanced core beliefs consolidated. Others marry those who fill in their gaps and unmet needs.

So, for example, a man who did not receive the loving care of his mother because she was unwilling or unable, seeks a wife who will put him front and centre. Not only is he looking for a wife, he is looking for a mother figure to take over all the female roles and give him that which he had been wanting throughout his childhood. He sees that her running around and bearing all the household responsibilities is an expression of love on her part. Nothing less will do.

Those children who were raised in a chaotic and disorganised family grow up longing for a setup where they can be in control and a household organised in the way they want. Such core beliefs, such rigid dreams and often times, exaggerated aims and expectations can drive a relationship downhill and cause a marriage to fall apart.

Some women, who never received positive attention from a male in their childhood, may marry very strong men to fill the gaps in their experiences and tend to marry hurriedly. This may be related to their low self-esteem. In their urgency to seek out love and affection, they search this through different means, not all of which are *halal* (lawful). The woman has such high expectations of love being the cure-all, that these marriages can suffer when reality hits with all its challenges and struggles and leaves her regretting her decision. Narcissistic personalities that are self-centred and egotistical will be attracted to less expressive and co-dependent people as this dynamic feeds off each other.

I cannot stress enough how important it is for the *mahram* (unmarriageable) males of the family to give and show excessive amounts of love, affection, attention and care to the females of the house. This builds their confidence, self-esteem and makes them feel secure and safe at home. This is an investment that will pay itself off in the form of stable personalities and stronger women who will make sensible life decisions. Young girls who haven't been nurtured in that way and haven't had their 'love tanks'[4] filled up adequately are prey to making decisions that they may regret later on in life. When a person is starved of affection, it is all too easy for them to fall for that one person that may have shown them some affection at some point. That affection is no guarantee of a contented and stable future, as I have all too often seen young girls come to me in later life and share how lack of affection by their fathers and brothers led them to be deceived by others outside the house that were willing to show them what they wanted. It is not a leap of imagination that these girls are likely to be used and abused in their marriages.

4 See Gary Chapman, The Five Languages of Love

The following case represents the story of many young girls and women who have been deprived of love and care and were deceived and tricked into thinking that the grass is greener on the other side.

Case Study: Emptiness

Her Background: Farzana grew up in a household where her father was undemonstrative. She recalls feeling empty, sad and lonely within the house.

Emotional Turbulence: At 16, she met a man who was married with 2 children who, in her words, made her feel "valuable, important and loved." She ran away from home and lived as the second wife of this man. When she subsequently fell pregnant and had a baby, the man left her with no financial support. Farzana was clearly used and abused but her need for affection blinded her to reality. She needed counselling to work on her self-esteem and strengthen her self-awareness in order to make more sustainable decisions for the future.

Adult Manifestations of Childhood Issues

Low Self-Esteem

Self-esteem is core to our very being. The lack of it, paired as it often is, with self-neglect, affects marital life, relationships with parents, children, neighbours, dynamics at work and even one's self-image.

Unfortunately, there is a lack of awareness about the topic and this is not paid enough attention when in fact, it may be the underlying reason for problems and growing struggles and also a symptom of scarring from the past. Bullying, abusive treatment, favouritism, 'replacing' a parent or sexual abuse buried deep in childhood memories are only some of the potential causes for poor self-esteem that develop in later age. This leads to people settling for poor and abusive conditions in a marital relationship, as co-dependents or people-pleasers. I go deeper into this pivotal issue of self-esteem in Chapter 4.

Lack of Emotion

It is commonly accepted than men are collectively the less emotional of the sexes than women, but one of the key complaints I hear of women is that their husbands seem unemotional and unresponsive. Some have never been affectionate or shown empathy for the feelings of their wives – perhaps they have not even known that is what they should be doing. This struggle to display and feel emotions is a symptom of something deeper.

Some cultures frown at the display of emotion by men and see this as a threat to their masculinity, so there is a generation of young men who have never seen a display of emotion or affection from their male relatives. They have no way of knowing that emotion is normal and natural and they have no template to follow.

Others experience emotional disconnection or lack of ability to connect emotionally due to harsh, angry parenting. They may have been told that, "Boys don't cry!" or to "Man up!" which leads them to be fine-tuned and programmed to suppress, neglect and overlook their emotional world. This suppression, avoidance or denial can even be the reason for frustration, anger or even hatred that has been left unexplained for them.

Emotional disconnection can also be a learned behaviour when dealing with struggles and hardship in the early years. These 'teach' the child that life is about survival and that is best achieved if emotions are switched off. This mechanism helps them to manage not being hurt over and over again; by burying their emotions away and pretending to be someone else, having opposite feelings or perhaps none and putting on a mask. As a survival strategy in a difficult time, it may be very useful but it is hard to know when to take the mask off and so the person is trapped in a pressure cooker of emotions that they do not know how to release.

Many high-functioning men may explain their inability to express emotions or emotionally connect through rationalisation or intellectualisation. These are some commonly used defence mechanisms especially known and embraced in psychodynamic counselling. However, this mechanism can be a shield behind which people can hide so as not to face and experience their inner true self.

Although I am focusing on men at the moment, this happens to women too, who can also develop a very rocky and hard shell of a façade, who speak a non-emotional language, and act and portray an image that seems to be free of emotional nuance. Yet the space inside that façade is not free of emotion at all.

Case Study: Switching off Emotions

His Background: Kashif's mother passed away when he was 6 years old. He has some very vivid memories of the emptiness. He remembers how everyone was grieving and the entire atmosphere in the family had changed dramatically. "It was never the same again!" he said sadly. "I would come home and there was no lunch or dinner again in our home which never happened when my mother was alive. It no longer felt like home for me." In time, his father remarried and things just got worse at home. Kashif was aware that things were never going to improve and he was convinced that he just needed to bury things away and pretend it was okay. He said, "I consciously made an effort to distance myself from my family, in fact from everybody. I remember many days I would come home from school, go up to my room, without saying a word to anyone. I had reduced interactions with my siblings too. I remember feeling cold and very isolated." Although he knew they were going through their own traumatic experiences, he didn't want to know. "All emotions became the same to me, I couldn't differentiate anymore," he told me. "I just got through the days as I had made up my mind to leave home as soon as I could."

Emotional Turbulence: Kashif became numb and unable to have a close relationship. Counselling helped him to reconnect with his feelings, sometimes by living through painful memories, but he is now able to enjoy a closer and loving relationship with his wife.

Although lack of emotion doesn't sound as serious as some of the other marital issues, it can be so extreme as to need help. I have had a woman come and see me complaining that, "Even when I would be curled up on the floor sobbing, he would just walk over me!" There **are** men like this, and that it is not only mental health, personality disorders or a traumatic experience that may be at play here, rather it is a learning disability or developmental health problem. Some of my clients have come back to me explaining to me that their husbands have been diagnosed with Autism and/or Asperger's Syndrome. While these specific health conditions need to be managed through the correct medical channels, there are coping strategies that can help ease the situation.

Case Study: Asperger's Syndrome

Emotional Turbulence: Maymuna and Abdul Majeed came to me as a couple who always argued. Maymuna's main complaint was, "His emotional intelligence is zero." Even as I saw her crying and sobbing, all I could see Abdul Majeed doing was to look at her, not knowing how he should react.

Diagnosis: I asked Maymuna and Abdul Majeed to visit their doctor and they came back with a diagnosis of Asperger's Syndrome. This was not only a relief for Abdul Majeed, it certainly helped Maymuna. Knowing that this behaviour wasn't deliberate and intended, she was able to take it less personally and this resulted in fewer arguments. The resultant energy was used to adjust to this condition and deal with it more constructively.

This case study shows us that even when the circumstances don't change as such, it is helpful to adjust the lens with which we view them and that can help our own emotional regulation.

Intimacy Issues

Abuse and traumas affect self-esteem, confidence, mental health and anxiety levels in various ways and impact the marital relationship. When it affects the intimate aspect of marital life, it can cause severe turbulence due to the spouse avoiding sexual and physical touch. Many people feel deeply uncomfortable talking about their past abusive experiences, particularly if they were sexual, and their pain remains buried away deep inside, trapped with shame and guilt. This can create bigger turmoil and friction at home as there is an underlying reason, a heavy baggage that is left unpacked and uncovered.

It is important to acknowledge the struggles and problems in the intimacy aspect of the marriage and address the issues appropriately. The struggles may be related to trauma and abuse, but sometimes other root causes such as physical illness, mental health illness or hormonal imbalances may lead to and trigger such difficulties. It is important to overcome the stigma and taboo surrounding this topic and be ready to seek help from professionals in the area of psychosexual health.

Anxiety

Many men and women in our community are of the belief that mental health issues only exist or are prevalent in those with low iman, those who sin frequently or may be possessed by jinn. The truth is that black magic and jinn do exist and some people are perhaps affected by them. I ask Allah to cure them and make their path easy. However, the stigma surrounding mental health and common disorders like anxiety are misunderstood and completely neglected. For this very reason, I want to take the opportunity to spend a little time with this condition that we all have seen in our families, friends, neighbours or experienced ourselves yet were unable to label, name or perhaps seek help for.

Anxiety is a real condition and completely unrelated to the level of iman that a person has. There are various subtypes, characteristics and criteria that help professionals to diagnose anxiety. Some of the main and most common anxiety disorders are panic disorders, obsessive compulsive disorders, social anxiety disorders, generalised anxiety disorders and post-traumatic stress disorder. These forms of anxiety can in fact persist and remain with the patient for many very difficult years and the suffering can in some cases be deeper and more difficult than some physical ailments. Anxiety disorders not only increase morbidity and mortality, they cause financial, career and social difficulties, severely reduce the quality of life and cause prolonged distress. The complexity lies in the fact that this is an invisible issue, and people think that the sufferer can just snap out of it if only they tried hard enough.

From my experience in counselling and work in the community, I can not only promise that there is hope, insha'Allah, I can easily say that seeking help from professionals in the fields of medicine and therapy makes a huge impact and speeds up the process of healing. There are also various drugs that are prescribed for anxiety. When people feel uncertain and worried about medication that they are prescribed by their doctors, they tend to ask those in their social circle for advice. It is worth bearing in mind that the community at large is not trained in healthcare and their knowledge can be blurred and inaccurate.

There is a misconception that every mental health drug causes weight gain, addiction and life long dependence. This can be true for some and very select drugs that not many healthcare professionals would opt for as the starting point. If you are a sufferer, I strongly recommend contacting your doctor or trusted therapist and work towards a trust-based relationship, exploring all the options that are available to you, which include:

- Psychological therapies including cognitive behavioural therapy (CBT), other behavioural therapy, analytical therapy, relaxation response training, and mindfulness meditation training;
- Talking therapies including psychodynamic, person-centred or integrative approaches;
- Drugs such as anti-depressants and anxiolytics can help you get back to a functional level if the condition is extremely debilitating. It takes a few weeks for the effects to show and this is not a quick fix solution. The hard self inner work still needs to be done.

The mind and body are tightly interlinked. The issues of the mind slowly diffuse into the body and manifest themselves in the physical arena, and the reverse is also true; the pains and struggles that affect the body also impact the mind in terms of mood, mental health and even emotional stability. Gaining an awareness of one can often facilitate healing in the other.

Feelings of anxiety can spill out into the body and show up as muscle tension, neck and shoulder stiffness and pain, fatigue and excessive tiredness, feelings of restlessness, disturbed sleep, concentration and focus struggles, consistent and disturbing worry, all of which are increasingly debilitating. For this reason, it is better to seek help sooner rather than later.

What you can do:

- Practise mindfulness by actively noticing what is happening in the present moment? What are the sensations you feel?
- Exercise regularly. This can be as simple as a 20 minute walk in your locality.
- Try focusing in your breathing. A suggested exercise is to breathe in for a count of four and to breathe out for a count of six.
- Reduce caffeine intake.

Anger

Anger is a really common problem across all the demographics, in women and men. It has various shades and different ways of showing itself from acting passively: ignoring someone or 'forgetting' something important to them or simply giving them the silent treatment; to being aggressive: verbally in terms of screaming and shouting or physically in throwing things, lashing out or actually hitting family members.

Case Study: Anger Problem

Emotional Turbulence: Asim openly admitted, "I have anger problems." His wife had explained he would spit at her and swear at her. He would constantly argue over the smallest issues and throughout the marriage, he had hit her quite a few times. Then I asked him, "You have accepted the fact that you have anger problems, let me ask you, where does this anger come from?"

His Background: Asim simply said, "This is what I saw growing up! This is what my father did to my mother."

His Core Belief: Holding on to anger became a comfort blanket for Asim and his unconscious mind made it acceptable as that is all that he knew. Interestingly and very importantly he would repeat, "I hate doing this, I don't want to do this and I want to get better!" So the comfort blanket was not comforting anymore but the action was familiar and known. It was this that needed to be changed. The familiar needed to be made unfamiliar.

There is an accepted narrative that the receivers of anger must be weak or uneducated or housewives or from 'back home', whether that anger was received as a child or is received as a spouse. However, traumatic experiences in childhood or abusive relationships aren't selective or particular to one type of economic or social background. It can happen to anyone if Allah chooses and destines this for His servant.

So where does all this anger come from? As we have seen from the case study, anger may arise because that is how situations were dealt with by our elders and the pattern is repeated decades later. It may also be fired up when someone feels threatened, because they perceive that their boundaries have been encroached or they do not get, what they perceive is, a need met.

Living or loving someone with anger management problems may always feel like walking on eggshells – daily life is unpredictable and uncertain. It is hard to know what will make them tick or explode, much like a volcano that may erupt at any point in time.

A small, seemingly irrelevant incident will suddenly escalate into something major. He comes home to find no salt in his dinner and suddenly he is swearing and spitting. She finds the bins haven't been taken out and begins shouting accusatory statements like, "You are so lazy. You never do anything around the house." From the very beginning, it was never about salt or rubbish. The smaller issue at the top of the heap has forced the entire pile of anger to avalanche down. Anger about something that happened in childhood, something the boss said, something the mother-in-law did.

Other people that suffer with this issue are continuously in that mode. They don't need to erupt suddenly. Their behaviour and attitude is based on constant anger and release of frustration. That is what marks their personality. Sometimes anger management problems can spiral out of control into hitting, kicking, punching, throwing things, swearing, breaking items. If issues escalate to a degree at which either yourself, someone else and especially children are in danger and targeted by such abusive behaviour, seeking help immediately is essential.

Some sufferers are conscious of what they are doing, and others seem like they have been taken over by a demon to the extent that they may lose presence and insight. In the case of narcissism, which we will look at in detail later on in this chapter, the perpetrator in addition to being severely angry, may blame their own anger on the spouse, children, work colleagues or the setting, thus justifying it in their own eyes.

What you can do:

- Recognise and identify what causes anger: tiredness, hunger, noise, the end of a long work day, deviation from routine etc.
- Work to avoid those triggers.
- If you find yourself having started a pointless argument, then both parties need to leave to cool off and gain perspective (not to ruminate about the faults of the other and feel worse and angrier). This will stop the situation escalating and is fine to do until both people can speak to each other rationally, as according to the hadith below:

Narrated Ibn 'Abbas ﵄ that the Prophet ﷺ said, "If any of you becomes angry, let him keep silent." (Ahmad)

- Reflect to see what the real reasons are below the top of the heap and address those.
- For more severe and prolonged bouts of anger, anger management counselling is a priority and key for the healing process.
- Seek refuge with Allah by saying *Audhu billahi minash shaytanir rajeem* as per the hadith below:

Narrated Sulaiman ibn Surad that the Messenger of Allah ﷺ said when he saw two men quarrelling, "Verily, I know a word he could say to calm himself: I seek refuge in Allah from the cursed Satan." (Bukhari and Muslim)

- Recite the Qur'an and increase remembrance of Allah throughout the day and at the moment of anger. Tranquillity, comfort and wisdom can only descend by the will of Allah and He alone is the One we need to call upon.
- Perform wudu:

Narrated 'Atiyyah that the Prophet ﷺ said, "Verily, anger comes from Satan and Satan was created from fire. Fire is extinguished with water, so if you become angry then perform ablution with water. (Abu Dawud)

- Changing position and thus changing perspective as advised by the hadith:

Narrated Abu Dharr ؓ that the Prophet ﷺ said, "If any of you becomes angry and he is standing, let him sit down, so his anger will go away; if it does not go away, let him lie down." (Ahmad)

This is a form of mindfulness practice, where we pause ourselves, calm our bodies and focus on thoughts and feelings.

The most excellent of advice in this matter is:

Narrated Abu Huraira ؓ that a man said to the Prophet ﷺ, "Advise me." He said, "Do not become angry." The man repeated his request several times, and each time the Prophet ﷺ told him, "Do not become angry." (Bukhari and Muslim)

In another narration, the very same man reflected on why the Prophet ﷺ offered him this advice and explained that he recognised anger as the combination of all evils (Ahmad).

Perhaps it is the beginning of many other evils. It certainly leaves mental, emotional, if not physical scars on the receiver and a Muslim should be someone from whose hands and tongue another is safe (Bukhari). Allah knows best what it does to us deep down and how it affects our hearts and minds, and most importantly our faith. It is part of our personal development and strengthening and the beautification of our moral conduct to focus on the control and management of our anger.

For this reason, we need to aim to clear out the anger that does exist within us for whatever underlying reasons and to shift our mindset so that external situations do not trigger us so easily. We must believe that this is an achievable goal otherwise our beloved Prophet Muhammad ﷺ would not have advised and recommended something that was impossible or against the *fitra* (natural innate character).

For those that can undergo a program of anger management coupled with forgiveness, they gain the pleasure of Allah as it is one of the qualities of the *Muhsinun* (the strivers of excellence), who are describe as those:

> ***Who spend [in the cause of Allah ﷻ during ease and hardship and who restrain anger and who pardon the people - and Allah loves the doers of good.*** (Surah Al-Imran 3:134)

Managing anger is not just for ourselves or our immediate families for the moment. Anger is recycled from generation to generation. No matter what teachings were imposed on us or that we teach our children, it is what is lived by the children that sticks in their minds. If they only see anger then like a rubber band that returns to its original size and shape, they will return to their original state of becoming their parent, of being whatever they saw and experienced in those formative years.

The cycle must be broken and if therapy is needed to do that, then this is what must be done. Angry parenting leads to:

- Children that have low self-esteem and all the baggage that entails. It is highly important for us to raise children that receive unconditional love, reassurance, acceptance where achievements and successes are not the deciding factor for happiness.
- Adults that are unsettled, angry, aggressive and impulsive individuals, or
- Adults that are people pleasers to avoid confrontation, that overcompensate and do not set any boundaries for their own children.

Both scenarios are equally unhealthy. They lead to different issues at different intensities yet the outcome is equally debilitating and disempowering as the following case study shows.

Case Study: Overcompensation in Parenting

Emotional Turbulence: Yasmin was exhausted because her children had became very disruptive in their behaviour. They were extremely needy and had stopped listening to even the smallest of requests. I asked her what her parenting style was. She replied, "I don't think I have any boundaries or any guidelines with my children. If I say no to something and they cry, straight away I give in and I give them whatever they want." Three children that are given whatever they want, whenever they want. No wonder she was exhausted!

Her Background: Yasmin grew up in a household where no one took proper care of her needs. She was overcompensating to fulfil every little desire of her children out of guilt. This is not a healthy parenting strategy and she learned in counselling about the difference between firm love for the benefit of the children and passive love which was really to their detriment and how to practise the former without guilt.

Not all anger stems from childhood. The anger between married couples arises from accumulated hurt feelings and broken expectations. These evolve over time to become frustrations and lashing out. The root of this anger is due to the care, love and expectation that spouses have of one another. It can be heart-breaking when those expectations are shattered. For example, if a husband sends an inappropriate text to a female work colleague, a wife will experience hurt, damaged trust and a deflated self-esteem. Her anger in this situation is different from an anger carried through from childhood. Of course, the two types of anger can co-exist in one person and compound. Healing would involve teasing apart the different angers that exist and working through these in turn.

Infidelity

When expectations and needs aren't met on an ongoing basis, both husband and wife are left feeling unfulfilled and try and find that fulfilment in different ways. When either spouse feels that they are not appreciated, thanked, loved, and respected the way they need to be, then it is all too easy to seek that attention from people outside the relationship that can range from a light flirtation through to the major sin of committing adultery.

Case Study: Glances

Her Background: Nabeel has stopped paying attention to Rubina even though she is still young and they have been married for a few years. He never looks at her or offers any affection or gives her any compliments.

Emotional Turbulence: Rubina confessed to me that she tries very hard not to look and exchange glances with men. She mentioned once she was sitting at a café with her friend and a man across the table caught her eye. She said, "Something in me told me I should look away but it was making me feel good about myself and happy. I started thinking that someone is still attracted to me and that I am still beautiful, so I kept looking." She continued, "I know this is wrong but if I was getting that attention, those looks, kind words and affection from my husband, perhaps I would not be seeking it elsewhere or struggle to control myself."

This is something that happens quite often. When needs and wants aren't met, often these are sought elsewhere even if it is completely inappropriate.

Husbands are also guilty of such behaviour. Wives express quite often that they find their husbands a bit more secretive on gadgets, or they have caught them looking at women and perhaps exchanging flirtatious messages. This is often seen in men as part of their mid-life crisis. It may mean and lead them to seek attention and get validation and prove that they are still attractive, able and capable of drawing attention. They may turn their attention to try to attract younger women just to prove this point. This is can also be linked to low self-esteem, in which case it is even more important that spouses keep paying each other positive attention.

Narcissism

One of the most damaging combination of couples that I see in my practice, is the narcissist who is married to the co-dependent. One of the reasons I wrote this book was to shed light on this type of relationship and disentangle the interwoven issues and struggles behind these marriages. A number of people feel trapped in these troubled marriages but never feel confident or knowledgeable enough to make an informed decision that will be for the better for everyone. So these marriages drag on, releasing toxicity, damaging the spouses, the children, the wider families but never reach a resolution. I have witnessed the pain, hurt and grief in these individuals, seen the scars on their children and feel the need to spend some time addressing this most complex of relationships.

In psychological terminology, it is commonly known as narcissistic personality disorder. Although statistics would suggest and research would argue it is rare and not too common, it is sadly one of the personality disorders I see too often in our community. Most of the time, narcissists are misperceived as selfish, arrogant and perhaps aggressive. None of these descriptions are wrong as such, but they are not strong enough. It is much more complex than that. The narcissistic person is convinced about their own self-importance and is overwhelmed by their greatness and ultimate superiority to others. This may not be verbally expressed at all times or to everyone, however, in intimate and close relationships, many of these traits come to light and appear frequently.

Narcissists are known to have a greatly distorted image of themselves and their self-belief is beyond what others think of them. This personality disorder convinces a person that their opinions and views are better, more significant and interesting than others'. They are self-absorbed and self-amazed. The world revolves so clearly around them that the traits of empathy, insight and introspection are almost non-existent in them. In fact they are recognised by their self-praising, exaggerated focus on themselves and their arrogant behaviour.

In relationships, this type of person is very patronising, insisting that things are done their way, on their schedule. If that doesn't happen, then there are bursts of anger and rage and extremely emotionally manipulative behaviour. Many of these behaviours are attention seeking as the narcissist has a strong urge to always be the centre of focus, to be better and above others.

In life purpose, they are unrealistic about themselves, their goals and their ambitions and usually set unrealistic targets and expectations of themselves.

This anger, self-amazement, aggression, self-centeredness, inclination to belittle, ridicule, criticise and be jealous (for no reason) can be lethal for a marital relationship, in fact for any relationship. All the relationships that a narcissist is part of are very unhealthy and very unstable, simply because the key aspects of a healthy relationship such as empathy, listening, compassion and love are just not part of the narcissist's tool box.

To add insult to injury, these people are very difficult to identify because they are high-functioning, meaning that they are good at masking their true self and can come across as charismatic and charming. A narcissist chooses his life partner intelligently: picking people who are vulnerable, coming from an abusive family home or people pleasing. Statistics suggest this is more prevalent in men than women, which I would probably agree with for the audience I deal with. Most of my clients are the wives of husbands that may have narcissistic traits.

The other thing that makes this disorder difficult to diagnose, identify and perhaps highlight is the fact that it is a spectrum. Some people are 'more' narcissistic than others. Thus everybody's narcissistic traits vary, are unique to themselves and appear at different intensities, but have only their unpredictability in common.

However, no matter where in the spectrum a person lies, any level of narcissistic personality disorder requires seeking professional help before the negative effects filter irrevocably down generations. We must be brutally honest in recognising narcissistic traits in ourselves and in our family members. For the mother that knows her son is narcissistic but insists that he marries that unsuspecting girl anyway, this is enabling an injustice. This process requires one to be strategic, kind, thoughtful and patient and to help our loved one through this trial because after all that has been said, there is within the self-absorbed person, a sensitive seed and a broken heart.

Behind the strong, ultra-confident and arrogant mask, they may hide and bury their low self-esteem and very disturbed image of themselves. There may be untouched fears and untold childhood traumas that are hidden away behind that exterior shield of protection. Whatever the causes for this personality disorder, be it genetic or as a result of environmental factors, ultimately the cause and cures are in the hands of Allah and we are only here to seek help through and from Him and do the best we can through all that He has equipped us with.

We can do our best to try the understand the factors that may lead to such a personality forming, if only to prevent those circumstances occurring to produce narcissists in the next generation. Childhood abuse, passive parenting, aggressive parenting, over pampering can all affect a child so greatly that their self-esteem is disturbed. So balance in all matters seems to be the prescription.

Narcissism can sometimes lead to alcohol or drug abuse, suicidal ideations and other mental health conditions that may result in physical abuse or domestic violence within the home. It is, therefore, not only the narcissist that needs healing, but anyone who has been close to one will not have escaped unscathed and will need healing as well.

What you can do:

- As a first port of call, I would recommend those married to a narcissist to schedule a visit to a doctor for a mental health assessment and then a therapist for the emotional healing element for their affected spouse and themselves. This is a process that requires patience, a strong support network, an optimistic outlook and the need to stick with a program of therapy. The unstable nature of the illness means that there are up and downs and it is vital not to leave therapy mid cycle until the emotional turbulence has settled.

- The aims and objectives of any treatment are to divert and shape the thinking and feeling pattern of the client to ensure that it results in the formation of a better and healthier self picture as well as more stable, healthy interactions and bonds with their social surroundings. Over time, the client may enjoy the improvements and come to realise there is more to life than all the inner battles they wake up to every day and close their eyes to every night. In reality, narcissism can be painful and a huge heart ache for the sufferer themself. Bearing this in mind can help the relative, spouse, friend and supporter of a sufferer.

With regards to counselling, the scenarios I see in my practice are fairly common. The wife will typically tell me that she has been married for years, how much she is suffering and that she doesn't know what to do because she is utterly exhausted. I ask her to describe her husband and she describes someone with the personality traits I have mentioned.

Case Study: Narcissistic Husband

Emotional Turbulence: Daniya told me, "My husband is very manipulative, tells lies, has a very arrogant and abusive way of dealing with the children. I cannot take it anymore. I can't see how my marriage can continue like this!" Zulfiqar refused to come to counselling and blamed Daniya for being a trouble maker and bad wife. Daniya could not continue any longer and went, with her children, to stay with her parents for 3 months. After this time, Zulfiqar realised that Daniya was serious and agreed to counselling as he did not want to lose his children. That time on his own made him realise there may be issues in him that he needed to deal with.

His Background: Zulfiqar spoke of his parents' lack of respect and appreciation when he was growing up that led him to feel undervalued. No matter what he did for his father, it was never good enough; he would always be criticised and put down. In this way, his self-esteem was destroyed by the time he was a young adult.

His Core Belief: His core belief became that in order to recover any sense of self, he needed to be the one in charge. And unfortunately, he did this through the tools he had learnt from his father: blaming, criticising, and ridiculing everyone else.

Solution: Through counselling, his hard work, doing his homework and trust in Allah, he became a stronger person and his relationship with Daniya and his children improved.

This case study shows that, if there is willingness, narcissistic personalities have the potential to improve. Through therapy, they can embark on a journey of healing that enables them to accept, develop insight and self-awareness, which in turn pushes them to make positive changes for themselves and their family. This is not an easy process but worthwhile if it breaks the cycle of narcissistic parenting.

By the will of Allah, there is much benefit in accepting the personality disorder and committing to healing through therapy. This is not something that can be managed alone. Of course, du'a and tawakkul play a key role in healing but this should always be done with seeking help through all permissible means possible.

The Co-Dependent Spouse

The spouse of the narcissist, is more often than not, a co-dependent personality. Co-dependent people may be easy to identify through their passive behaviour and thoughts, or their inclination to always worry about and prioritise others' needs. They might have a tendency to always try and do more and more and it is usually never about them. It is almost as though they have decided to live a life that is based on sacrificing all that is important for them.

If such a personality type is in a relationship with a narcissistic person who is perhaps suffering with anger management problems too, then there is the potential for a highly imbalanced marriage. The co-dependent person starts becoming very cautious to ensure they accommodate the needs and demands of the narcissistic person. Their behaviour, words, posture and gaze all align to appease the narcissist, to bend over backwards to accommodate them for fear that they start being abusive, verbally or physically. That fear and heightened state of stress convert into severe levels of anxiety, panic attacks and many other mental health conditions. Co-dependents may be likely to avoid situations that test boundaries and confrontation. Their self-image and sense of self-worth can be much distorted and damaged. Although their body may need and desperately yearn for some attention and quality care, their system has not been given it for so long that it cries out in pain and illness. No wonder the co-dependent becomes exhausted. The narcissist is too absorbed to see what they are doing to their spouse. I like to describe it as the narcissist being the spider and the co-dependent being the fly in the web.

Ironically, the reasons for developing a co-dependent personality may be similar to the ones that create a narcissistic one. Many co-dependents come from a family background that provided an environment of repression, oppression and perhaps a degree of neglect. It is not uncommon for clients to deny or refuse these experiences; sometimes they open up about these facts many sessions later. I have seen and witnessed a deep and very heavy sense of guilt, blame and shame in these people. They think they are the reason for everything that goes wrong or may go wrong. Their anger is slightly passive, commonly inward-directed yet present and very common. One of the major reasons for negative self-image and low self-esteem in co-dependents is the constant negative self talk. Being self-critical has become part of their understanding of their way of functioning and some people cannot accept compliments, praise, good treatment, gifts or anything similar. In their head, there are many should-haves and could-haves and high expectations of themselves and a sense of "I'm not good enough to deserve anything better." There is confusion between being obedient and patient, and being oppressed and being tortured in a relationship.

The scholars of Islam are unanimous: abuse and oppression have no place in a marriage. According to the Qur'an, the marital relationship is based on love and mercy, comfort and mutual protection (Surah 30:21 and Surah 2:187). It is NEVER part of a spouse's duty or obligation to remain passive or accept abuse. This is the case whether the abused spouse is male or female.

Co-dependents often have a sense of perfectionism that follows them through life, which doesn't give them the space to relax. Rather, they spend their life being too afraid and worried about 'failing' and 'making mistakes'. Through counselling, this submissive mindset can be released and very often people can be propelled to achieve their full potential in a healthy way that is neither submissive nor aggressive.

Case Study: Co-dependency

Emotional Turbulence: Sajida has been in an abusive marriage for 8 years. She is not only abused by her husband but also her in-laws. She is abused and oppressed financially and made to give all her own earnings back to the family. Her relationship is about the family; she does not have privacy and a healthy sustainable relationship with her husband. Her husband has full control of her time, she isn't allowed to meet any of her friends, and she is kept so busy at home that she does not have time for herself. Her marriage is based on threats and severe aggression and everything has to be done her husband's way. He insists his parents are always right and she is wrong by criticising and belittling her.

Her Core Belief: Sajida is depressed and imprisoned and feels like she lives the life of a servant. Her core belief is that she is worthless and has no value.

Solution: Through therapy, she has learnt to recognise narcissistic behaviour and abuse, to consider why she was absorbing this treatment and to give voice to her thoughts. This is a key step in identifying the issues that need to be dealt with, otherwise unspoken thoughts simply remain inside the head. Therapy has helped her to feel empowered by having knowledge of the situation, to put coping strategies in place and deal with the situation constructively. We discovered that her father had been a similar personality and that is why she became the way she did. Counselling helped her rethink her core beliefs and come up with a long term strategy that is positive and constructive.

In the end, masha'Allah, Sajida was empowered enough to come up with her own solutions, moving from co-dependence to independence. She became strong enough to set boundaries, prioritise herself and make independent decisions for her safety, well-being and good mental health. During the course of those months of counselling, Sajida's complexion, posture and language all changed for the better, alhamdulillah.

Co-dependent personalities are usually individuals who have been subject to some sort of abuse, trauma, and 'enslavement' in their past so that when they meet a narcissistic personality, they are the 'perfect prey'. This process of choosing each other or being attracted to each other is never premeditated, it may just be that we are attracted to personalities that we are familiar with (see Chapter 2). Co-dependent individuals are typically identifiable as people pleasing, slightly anxious and very sensitive individuals who are likely to neglect themselves and their likes and dislikes and develop a deep focus and care for others, namely, the narcissistic person.

Narcissists often push the blame on others, "It's not my problem, you are the problem, you need counselling!", "If you were more [this] or less [that], I wouldn't need to be this way." Even when they recognise certain issues within themself, the narcissistic person can still be very defensive, likely wanting to stop therapy or end the relationship.

The common denominator amongst co-dependent individuals is their past and the existence of negative, toxic and abusive environments and very shaky, unstable and 'disturbing' relationships. Abuse, continuous criticism, badmouthing, comparison with others and 'labelling performance' as underachieving are some of the destroyers of the self-worth of such children. From then onwards, nothing may work out for them, and that is the perception they usually hold of themselves too.

Case Study: Co-dependency 2

Emotional Turbulence: When I met Safura, her head was bowed and her whole being gave the message, "I am destroyed, hurt and broken." The more I looked at her, the more she spoke (not only in words but through her body language), I could hear the unspoken plea, "I am in pieces, torn apart; I have lost myself. Help!" Her broken posture was indicative of how close she was to a nervous breakdown. She struggled to speak, she seemed unfocused and was constantly apologising for everything she was sharing. It was clear that this was how she always was. Her 'Sorry' would come out so naturally and so emphatically. She genuinely was sorry and was in the belief that everything was her fault.

Fourteen years into her marriage, she found out that her husband had taken a second wife without her knowledge. As the mother of his three children, she parented them and looked after the house. He was not present in any way: physically, emotionally or financially. Through this, Safura was frantically searching in her mind, "I should have done...", "Perhaps I should have tried more", "Perhaps I should try harder." Whenever Usman would come home, he started blaming her, accusing and degrading her with words, looks and actions. He actually told her she was not worthy of anything.

Through the counselling sessions, we explored and identified that Safura was married to a man who may have some narcissistic traits. His greatest weapons seemed like control, obsession, and the power over her mind. He sounded very manipulative and knew precisely how to control her thoughts, feelings and responses. "Why are you not in that corner that I put you?" This form of abuse leads to a spouse having a very broken and unhealthy sense of self-esteem.

His Background: Usman was brought up spoiled by his parents and encouraged in his bullish behaviour to others. He was always obsessed with authority and control.

His Core Belief: Usman genuinely believed that the world revolved around him and his demands.

Her Background: Safura revealed that she was brought up in a home with critical parenting where she was unable to satisfy the expectations of her parents. She was never 'good' enough or worthy of respect, care or loving words. She grew up wanting some of the most basic emotional nutrients. She became an adult that was people pleasing, with the aim of being accepted and recognised. In her relationship, she became the co-dependent that wanted acknowledgement, yet was used and programmed to victimising herself. She felt comfortable and knew that role very well so did not struggle to embrace it.

Her Core Belief: "I am not good enough, I don't deserve to be treated well. It's my fault."

Solution: I cannot forget the moment when I told Safura, "It is not your fault, your husband would have been like this no matter whom and how his wife would have been." I cannot describe the surprise and happiness on her face when I explained to her what was happening in her relationship and why her husband may have that particular behaviour and attitude. It was a big relief for Safura. All this time, all she needed to hear was, "It's not your fault." This was the pivotal point after which Safura was able to shift her mindset and focus on self-care without guilt.

Co-dependents are likely to be the caretakers and empaths. Empathy is not a bad quality at all, but for the co-dependent, their level of empathy can become debilitating and an obstacle to self-care. Empaths are magnetically drawn towards narcissists and often they don't fully understand the reason for this attraction. The reason may be that narcissists are wounded and empaths are compassionate healers, and the two naturally gravitate towards each other. Empaths are sensitive to emotions and feelings, not only their own but especially others'. They have a constant desire to heal, soothe and improve others and their emotional state. Their attraction to narcissists may stem from their own perception that narcissists are in pain, in deep need of healing and improvement. Their focus on healing others is a medium they utilise to heal themselves; they relieve their own pain through their focus on others' pain.

It is important for the empath to bear in mind that the only person that can help and heal a wound is the owner and possessor of the wound. No external force, person or carer can take ownership and responsibility for someone else's wound. You may feel in charge, responsible and able to heal the narcissist in their surroundings, when in reality the only and most powerful thing you can do is to support the narcissist that is willing and interested in healing. This may be incredibly difficult to accept but the power of healing, making someone happier, more content or settled is not in the hands of anyone except themselves.

Children of Narcissistic/Co-Dependent Parents

Children who grow up in severe turbulence and unsettled circumstances, tend to suffer from anxiety. Many become isolated individuals and may suffer from eating disorders or issues such as bedwetting. These are just symptoms and we need to reflect on the root cause of those symptoms.

Part of counselling married couples is to explore the effects of their relationship on their child(ren) and to identify how the child's behaviour has been impacted by certain dysfunctional aspects of their parents' marriage. As parents, naturally we have our struggles and issues, but we need to work out how to resolve these with grace and faith, not by leaving deep scars on our children.

Children are known to practice mirror-learning which is essentially copying one of the parents and applying that same behaviour and attitude to the other parent. It is common to see a child that starts disrespecting their mother or father due to the behaviour of the other parent towards their spouse. The eldest child is usually the most affected and influenced and may end up carrying the heaviest emotional baggage. This is the case in most parenting scenarios as the eldest child is more exposed to parental challenges than siblings lower down the birth order.

These children develop a range of defence mechanisms to survive: some use the laughter card, and become the class clown to hide and mask the pain; others choose to avoid what is happening and perhaps turn inward and develop a hypersensitive and quiet personality. There is always an accumulation of various forms of anger which may be passive, implosive or explosive that can lead to disruptive behaviour and poor social interactions, difficulty making friends and maintaining bonds. Unfortunately, such children are also predisposed to become future narcissists or co-dependent mothers/fathers or just individuals who are poorly functional in their community and life.

What you can do:

There are some strategies or coping mechanisms that can be implemented by the co-dependent in dealing with their narcissistic spouse. Insha'Allah these go a little way to stabilising family life:

- **Stepping outside the box**: Take a step back and look at the problem from the outside. This can give you the space and time you need to calm down, reflect and think clearly and proactively rather than reactively.
- **Stepping away from the drama**: You do not have to jump on the emotional roller coaster that your spouse is on. This means recognising that their drama and emotional baggage is not yours and firmly being able to draw that line by not getting involved in the emotional and dramatic ups and downs. This is not easy if you have grown up in a household where drama was a key ingredient of daily life. However, it is something that takes practice and becomes easier and more natural with experience.
- **Emotional Detachment**: "It is not your fault." This is a key point and absolutely crucial to internalise if you

don't want to drown in the sea of emotion of your spouse. The example I give my clients is that if you married a person with asthma and they had episodes of breathlessness and needed their inhaler, would you blame yourself for their attack? You would accept this as part of their illness without feeling blame or guilt.

- **Disowning the 'negative emotions'**: This is about giving negative emotions and feelings back to the owner and telling them, "I am sorry you feel that way!" and not dwelling on it any further. It is about not getting emotionally involved and invested so that you do not end up being depleted energetically. It may sound uncaring, but this is about showing care, presence and kindness without direct involvement.
- **Applying diffusion techniques and phrases**: These are the phrases and techniques you can use to help get your message across, with firmness and which will help prevent the situation from escalating, insha'Allah:
  - "I guess we don't agree about this subject."
  - "It's okay with me that we just don't see eye to eye about this particular matter."
  - "I would appreciate if you would not disrespect me in this manner."
  - "I will not be manipulated into agreeing with you while you are screaming and shouting at me."
  - Try to remain calm and in control. This may need you to breathe consciously.
  - Guard your boundaries and have a dignified exit strategy in place.
  - Recognise the trigger points.

- Never accept blame. A common tactic is for you to be told that this is your fault and you started this, if only you had listened and done this or that, and so on. This is not true.
- Reflect on what is keeping you in this toxic relationship.

Domestic Violence

Domestic Violence (DV) as a term is used to describe any form of abuse that occurs within the context of a familial or intimate relationship. It need not be limited to being inside the home and includes, but is not limited to physical, emotional, verbal and sexual abuse. DV occurs in all cross-sections of life and affects men, women and children of all ages and backgrounds. It is not just a western phenomenon, or an Asian or an Arab or a Muslim problem. People of all nationalities, classes and religions have encountered this issue.

This is not something that Islam condones. Any form of oppression and physical violence is not permissible. This is a serious form of abuse that is not to be accepted, avoided or normalised. The Prophet ﷺ never hit a female and strongly emphasised that, *"The best of men are those who are best to their women."* (Tirmidhi)

DV instils and creates a very strong cycle of silence and fear that, in order to conquer, requires acknowledgement, acceptance and then step-by-step action. First of all, you have to break the cycle and seek help from organisations who work to reach out to sufferers of DV and aid them in seeking refuge and escape as well as healing. Furthermore, a program of recovery that involves therapy is vital in order to regain a sense of self worth.

I cannot highlight enough how clients of mine who sought help and advice through their doctors, organisations, charities or talking therapies have benefited immensely and made a drastic change to their quality of lives, themselves, their children and surely the generations to come after, by the grace of Allah. These were the very women who once thought there was no hope and no way out.

It is imperative that you seek help if you are suffering from domestic violence.[5]

Despondency

One of the side effects of going through extreme life challenges is that it does affect the relationship with Allah. There is a feeling of anger and hopelessness directed to Allah. No one likes feeling this way or wants to have these thoughts about Allah, but people describe feeling a loss of trust in Allah and worrying about their faith. This can be very disturbing as faith is often one of the few resources left to someone when all else seems to be going wrong. At an advanced stage, hopelessness may look like giving up, self harm, suicidal ideation or suicide attempts.

It can be difficult to acknowledge these feelings and can be some of the hardest things to admit to someone else, especially another Muslim. These feelings are symptoms of trauma, neglect, lack of interest, feelings of abandonment, loneliness and so on. They may also be coupled with anxiety. We are human and we have emotional responses to life challenges. Our job is to try to manage those emotional responses in a positive, accepting and healthy way or to get help in doing so.

5 Rahmanara Chowdhury, The Road to Recovery: Healing from Domestic violence, Ta-Ha Publishers

Suicidal Ideations

Sadly, this is more common than anyone in our community can imagine. Suicide itself remains such a devastating event for families and communities, leaving loved ones with guilt, shame, anger and a barrage of so many conflicting emotions that can fluctuate all the time. Current statistics suggest that there are more than 5,000 suicides in the UK and Ireland each year. That means one death every few hours. Despite the many efforts and charities working on raising awareness, introducing helplines and workshops, the figures seem to be increasing.

Perhaps one of the main reasons for this is the lack of reaching out to the 'affected' communities, and the lack of communication within families and society surrounding this topic. We have the added layer that religious beliefs can act as an obstacle to enabling sufferers to open up and share ideations, thoughts and plans. Suicide is still the leading cause of death amongst young people and is known to be higher in males – there are four times more men dying by suicide than women. Perhaps this may be linked to men being less likely to reach out for help in a timely manner. This goes back to the narrative in some quarters that men should not be emotional, so these men put emotions away very early in their development as they think it is a sign of weakness or associated with too much pain. They are less likely to speak out about their plans and are more likely to go through with them because nobody knew or could ask for help or create a support network at the right time.

Suicide and suicidal ideation are severely stigmatised and few who die by this method ever express their intentions of doing so to health professionals. This may be related to accessibility, with the focus of primary care being physical health rather than mental, or perhaps as simple as not being asked the right questions. The stigma is heavier within the Muslim community. Suicidal ideations are not expressed because of the judgement that the sufferer has weak iman or is not strong enough. Any feelings that are expressed are met with religious verdicts and reminders, where understanding and exploration are needed.

Some of the factors that are known to be associated with risk of suicide are poor social or financial conditions, unemployment, traumatic experiences or abuse, drugs, addictions and alcohol misuse, background in prison, violence, loneliness, other mental health issues and breakdown in marriages or families. These factors are found commonly in our community too.

It is vital to reach out and talk when such thoughts strike. They do not have to be dealt with alone and they are not to be dealt by criticising a person's faith or by quoting religious books.

Case Study: Hopelessness

Emotional Turbulence: Hanifa felt like a soul filled with hopelessness. Initially she spoke of her lack of hope, not having a vision for the future, not having any positive thoughts or expectations of herself. It took many sessions for her to be able to share that she no longer wished to continue living.

Her Background: In her words, she "messed up" her A-levels. Her father is abusive, degrading, aggressive and highly critical. He was furious that she did not get into university, which is something that she also wanted for herself.

Solutions: Through counselling, we explored her traumatic life experiences, self beliefs and focused on her academic performance and potential. Alhamdulillah, Hanifa has now started university.

Addiction

There are various forms of addictions and some of the prevalent ones are gambling, pornography, drugs, alcohol, smoking, shopping and computer games. Some are more common in men and others are more common in women.

Although some of the addictions mentioned above may come across as less harmful or distressing than others, the reality is that in the world of psychology and mental health, they are recognised as an illness that requires therapy, professional help and in some cases, medication and hospitalisation.

Addictions, especially those that are longstanding, do not just destroy the sufferer but affect their friends and family. They are very debilitating yet so easy to fall into because they offer distraction from pain, an increase in illusionary self-esteem and momentary pleasure. It is so easy to lose control, despite what the sufferer may believe of themselves, because addictions gather momentum, increasing in their intensity of damage and destruction with time, if left unchecked.

The starting point of an addiction is to forget, distract, escape and perhaps numb difficult feelings in certain situations. This may be facilitated by peer pressure. Then, over time, biochemical changes occur in the 'pleasure centres' of the brain which distort understanding of fun, joy, pleasure and good times. The brain then has trouble attaining pleasure through 'normal' means and needs increasing amounts of the addictive substance to reach that same 'high'.

Addictions require professional, medical and therapeutic help and, most importantly, more awareness in our community. An addict cannot just stop or exert willpower to stop being addicted. Their very brain chemistry is altered and this is an illness that needs treatment.

Often the addicts themselves may not admit they have a problem. They are convinced that they are a recreational addict who is just dabbling for fun and can stop whenever they choose. This is a reality that the addict creates for themself in order to cope with the reality of being addicted, which is lonely and debilitating.

Case Study: Gambling

Emotional Turbulence: Naseer was struggling with gambling and was spending the family income on online sites. His wife had begged him to seek help for the addiction as their marriage was suffering. Naseer denied that there was a problem. It was only when his wife threatened to leave that he sought help.

He explained, "The thoughts in my mind are overwhelming. They take up every waking moment in my life. They cram my brain like a tin of sardines and my head feels like it will burst. Someone will be talking to me, but I can't hear what they are saying to me. It's like I'm somewhere else, and cut off. Gambling gives me a break and a distraction from all that is going on in my head."

His Background: Naseer's father walked out when he was young and as the eldest sibling, he felt the weight of responsibility in looking after his mother and siblings. Since the day his father walked out, no one mentioned the incident. He says he felt shame and guilt over this.

Solution: We unpacked some of the thoughts in his head, his lack of direction, his anxieties and the excessive pressures on him and slowly, with the help of addiction organisations as well as family support, Naseer has begun to regain control of his life and gambling.

I will reiterate that this an issue of altered brain chemistry and no amount of willpower can overcome this. We as a community of mothers, fathers, siblings and spouses need to become more educated on the matter, and not shy away from confronting addictions, addicts and addictive behaviours or personalities. If we find our loved ones are affected we need to make an active effort to read up on these matters, ask professionals, contact services and go to awareness events and workshops to acquire tools and techniques to understand and cope with addiction, addicts and offer adequate support.[6]

Pornography

Pornography is a rising problem in our community amongst both males and females for reasons of distraction, numbing or forgetting painful feelings, suppressing or dealing with desires that cannot be fulfilled in halal ways, and/or peer pressure. Often the true reasons are only known to the person and this is one of those addictions that is only flagged up in a marital context when a spouse complains because their partner is always secretively on a device or perhaps left something open on a laptop inadvertently. In some cases, a person who is addicted to pornography may decide to seek help simply due to the internal conflict of knowing it is *haram* (unlawful), and causes the diseases of the heart to grow and infect the soul and mind.

It is a huge problem in many ways as it distorts self-esteem, causes behavioural issues, withdrawal, isolation and leads to debilitation of social life and functioning of the individual. It also impacts the marital relationship, in some cases leading to fertility problems, and deeper issues in intimacy with the spouse.

6 Yunus P, Hope for the Muslim Alcoholic, Ta-Ha Publishers

It can change and set difficult, in many cases, inappropriate and unacceptable, expectations from the spouse, or play with the self-esteem of the person who is addicted. Competing with unrealistic and exaggerated looks, performance and experience of on-screen material only leads to disappointment with reality, which keeps the addict in their online world.

Pornography is a multibillion dollar industry that is invested in, commercialised and spread everywhere. It starts with seemingly harmless bill boards, advertisements, films, online pop-ups of slightly suggestive material in the name of being liberated and expressive. Over time, these 'smaller' violations of our sight, hearing and time break down our modesty and normalise haram. Then it is just a matter of time before the 'smaller' harams become 'bigger' harams.

It reaches a point that whenever a person needs a place of escape, whenever they are in distress or overwhelmed or confused, they go to their device. It is so readily available and free and can be done in the comfort of one's own home in secret.

Intimacy is such a core part of the marital relationship, that when it is affected and/or not pleasing to one or both of the parties, it can affect the marriage in other areas. Sometimes, struggles in intimacy can lead to arguments and resentments that come up and appear in other ways and the deeper upset feelings about intimacy remain uncovered.

While these things cannot be predicted, it is a common pattern that young people left alone for too long or too frequently in their childhood may fall into such illnesses and become addicted. This does not mean that everyone that spends time alone or is going through a lonely period will fall into such things, however, this is something to be mindful of. Similarly, many teenagers start engaging in such activities due to curiosity, perhaps at boarding school. Peer pressure or friends discussing and normalising this can be, for many young adults, the first place and time for them to be interested and experiment and many years later find themselves as addicts that cannot enjoy anything else but that or struggle to fight that deeper drive for the 'thrill of the moment'. As with any other addiction, it needs professional help.

Barriers to Escape

These then are just some of the weighty issues that challenge marriages and they can be resolved with help and determination and tawakkul. So why do people struggle to seek help or change their circumstances?

It takes a lot of courage, and very strong determination to decide to take ownership of a difficult situation. You may be depleted from your challenges and cannot contemplate the effort it takes to change. When you are enveloped by your problems, it is difficult to know who to reach out to or how. Where do you begin to explain? The mountain seems too tall to climb.

However, there is a bit more than just courage, ownership, leadership and decisiveness at hand. Unfortunately, there are barriers other than your own feelings and emotions.

Some cultures have made it the norm for one gender to be submissive, not to be the troublemakers, to do their duty without complaint or emotion or expression. In fact, they are expected to be grateful for all they have been given and that it is not worse. Culturally, these individuals may be convinced they have to look good outside and everyone has to be of the belief that everything is going well and there is no issue. The key concern that families have is what people will say and think. This overrides any concern that someone may be suffering and victimised inside the walls of this 'perfect' family façade.

Negative patience can be the issue itself. Some people recognise that there are elements of abuse but prefer to label themselves as the victim and make themselves believe that their silence is patience and thus *ibadah* (worship). It is important to remind ourselves that tawakkul entails that it is a part of faith that we do everything possible to save and progress ourself alongside du'a and a deep reliance on Allah.

Next Steps

Pain, sorrow and deep sadness can all be ways in which we draw closer to Allah and increase in our reliance of Him.

- Read and reflect on Surah al-Anbiya (21). It is a very powerful chapter that reminds us of how many Prophets experienced distress on different levels, at various intensities and suffered from so many different angles. Surely, we can relate to at least one of these experiences. It may be illness like Ayyub ﵇ or being trapped like Yunus ﵇ or feeling alone during childbirth like Maryam عليها السلام. Our Lord is the One that commanded the fire to be coolness and safety for Ibrahim ﵇. How can we ever think that anything is beyond our Lord? But for that we have to act. We have to act to show our intention and then Allah helps us manifold. Patience is not just about waiting with no increase in belief, tawakkul or increased efforts to try.
- So many times in this Surah alone, Allah repeats, "And we responded to Him and we gave him Yahya" (21:90), "And we responded to him and we removed his distress" (21:84), "So We responded to him and removed

what afflicted him of adversity (21:85)." What is Allah responding to in these cases? He is responding to the du'a of these Prophets combined with action in that direction. Our patience is with increased and intense running back to Allah and seeking his aid whilst continuing to function productively and effectively.

Thinking about it, many of the Prophets mentioned in the Qur'an were disadvantaged children and had challenges as adults. Not only did they experience the most difficult trials, abuse and trauma, they were also the ones that struggled with others and mostly suffered from not being supported. Yet they were the selected and chosen ones that displayed the best of conduct, the best of character and the best of worship and they will enjoy the best of rewards for making the effort. In addition to the Prophets in the Qur'an, there are the female role models of Sara, Hajar, Maryam, Asiya (peace be on them all), Khadijah, Fatima and Aisha (may Allah be pleased with them all) amongst many other believing women.

They are all great because they did not cower in the face of challenge and the most extreme difficulties. Yes, they were afraid. Yes, they felt that they could not go on. They had the emotions that we have, but they still held on. Insha'Allah, when we call out, Allah will respond. This should be an incredible motivation and reason to hold onto the deen and strive for the best of outcomes.

Chapter 4

Self-Esteem

It would be no exaggeration to say that the essence of this book is self-esteem. Self-esteem is a buzz word these days. It's on everyone's lips, but the questions to ask are: how do we boost our self-esteem and what can we do to make a change in the next generation? When self-esteem is distorted and weak, it affects every part of life. It is the very foundation of any healthy and functional, productive relationship and, in particular, married life. So what exactly do we mean when we talk of self-esteem?

What is Self-Esteem?

Self-esteem is the acceptance of yourself and a deep sense of love for your own skills, achievements, limitations and beliefs – the whole package. The core of it is formed by the belief of our own self-importance. This is a belief that is encouraged by our Creator. We are reminded in the Qur'an to remember our purpose and significance and this mindset is very strongly intertwined with strong self-esteem. It is a belief that we are worthy and valuable, which allows us to be the best version of ourselves that Allah intended for us when He created us. This is not the same as arrogance. We have to recognise the difference between humility and low self-esteem.

Our obligation of humility is towards Allah and we display and live it by utilising our Allah-given talents in the most productive way for Him and for society at large. We show gratitude to Allah multiple times a day for all that we are and all that we have, even those not so pleasant experiences and characteristics, because we recognise Allah's wisdom and mercy in everything. We recognise that our growth and development depends on our unique set of circumstances and resources. Low self-esteem, on the other hand, is based on the rejection, neglect and overlooking of all the good, worthy and important parts of oneself that Allah has blessed us with. So, it is clear to see that low self-esteem is, in fact, the antithesis of humility.

Why is Self-Esteem Important in Islam?

While most people would recognise that healthy self-esteem is a vital ingredient to a healthy lifestyle and self-belief, not many people are aware that this is also key to our relationship with our Creator.

Individuals who have high self-esteem are more stable and less likely to be easily swayed and controlled by others. That is because they have direction, a firm healthy opinion of themselves coupled with unswerving principles and values – a purpose. Such people find it easier to be steadfast and stay on the Straight Path. So self-esteem is crucial in developing a strong connection with Allah and acknowledging the gifts and blessings that He has bestowed upon us. We are created for a lofty purpose, with beautiful and mind-blowing talents, we are worth it and most importantly, we are enough.

What is Low Self-Esteem and How Does it Develop?

The danger and the struggle with low self-esteem is the stealth of its nature. It does not have to be apparent nor is it low in a particularly identifiable group of people. It is not necessarily low-achieving, low income or lonely people that suffer from it; many high-achieving individuals are crippled by it. So how do you recognise it in yourself?

Some indications are: that you doubt yourself, you seek to please others even when that feels uncomfortable, you tend to sabotage positive thoughts and hold onto negative ones, you feel like you are not enough, you fear that you will fail. The thoughts that accompany this will sound like:

- "I'm not very clever"
- "I'm not really good for that"
- "I don't deserve that"
- "I blame myself for how that went"
- "I am too scared to try that" and so on.

This is negative self-talk, which can also take the form of "If only..." statements:

- "If only I was more beautiful, my husband would treat me better"
- "If only I was slimmer, I would have more friends"
- "If only I had more confidence, I would be able to do public speaking"
- "If only I wasn't stupid then I wouldn't fail all the time."

A negative self-image feeds on something that is already quite vulnerable. It's an emotional hole; a point of weakness inside you. All this negative self-talk, these critical thoughts and "If only..." statements are like taking a hammer and making that hole bigger. When something happens, you add a negative thought to your self, which lowers your self-esteem and you are more likely to make the same mistake again and so the negative cycle continues.

This is not simply the preserve of women either. Men also suffer from low self-esteem, and where low self-esteem exists, there is also likely to be lack of motivation, drive, lack of focus, severe forms of procrastination and indecisiveness and follow through on actions. When a young man embarks on a journey through therapy, it only takes us a very short while to uncover, for example, a father figure that may have been authoritarian, taking over his life and ruling with dictatorship. This not only takes away choices, wishes and dreams; it reduces the life energy, motivation and enjoyment of future steps.

Parents do not recognise what they take away from their children when they become possessive and obsessive over their children's next steps – the way they stand, walk, and make friends, and major decisions that affect how they are going to function as individuals. All that happens is that home becomes a hell rather than a haven and this means that any outside influence now has more power simply as a means of escape from home. The following are just some of the childhood reasons that people have low self-esteem as adults:

- **Comparison**: When children are compared to others, this distorts their beliefs about themselves and diminishes their value.
- **Being bullied**: This creates a big dent in the life of the child and continues to affect them in their adulthood. Victims of bullying may develop a strong sense of self-hatred and negative self-image of themselves.

- **Expectations:** Having unrealistic expectations of children, perhaps related to their studies and academia, or perhaps Islamic education, memorisation or even general conduct. Our worth is never dependent on the results we produce.
- **Verbal Abuse:** Being belittled, sworn at and being called names.
- **Emotional Neglect**
- **Sexual and Physical Abuse**

Once self-esteem has been damaged and the deprecating narrative has been put in place, the self-criticising and negative self-talk only increases and over time, people can become their own worst enemies. Where others once put constraints on them, people put constraints on themselves. Even as adults, they echo the negative language that was spoken to them as children. However, it is never too late to develop a shift in mindset.

I am not saying this to incite resentment or anger with parents but if they have induced various instabilities, insecurities and wishes that were never fulfilled, eventually leading to low self-esteem, we need to recognise this with grace. There will invariably have been circumstances that led our parents to parent this way – that is not for us to judge. But it is for us to break the cycle for own children. If we love them as much as we say we do, then this is something we must focus on.

Looking into our parental background, we may find deep-rooted traumas that gave rise to our parents' understanding of parenting, relationships and, in some cases, they may even genuinely have thought they were offering the best they could. If they weren't exposed to love and affection and weren't nurtured with deep care and love, how could they know how to mould their parenting with these feelings? Our parents often experienced the death of one or both of their parents at younger ages than we commonly do now, so where were their role models?

Identifying reasons and root causes for why our parents are the way they are, will help us to have more compassion and empathy for them, help us to be more affectionate with them, develop an understanding, forgiveness and through this, of course, our relationship with them will improve. This is part of pleasing Allah as we know the great importance that our Lord puts and places on being good to our parents. We can only have and develop wings of mercy and duty to our parents if our own healing has started and forgiveness and affection has been added to our heart. When we are filled with these qualities, they can be passed to our children, insha'Allah.

As I touched on in the previous chapter in the section on infidelity, low self-esteem can also manifest itself as inappropriate behaviour and desire to seek attention from the opposite sex. Some people who suffer from low self-esteem have been feeling guilty of this behaviour and describe that they entertain and enjoy the attentions of someone other than their spouse. This temporarily makes them feel good about themselves as they regain some belief in their beauty and capacity to attract. Husbands and wives often say that if they got any kind of attention at home, they would not do this. Although this type of behaviour cannot be justified by a lack of attention, affection and kind words, it highlights that spouses need to make the effort to be kind and attentive with one another. Not doing so, not only harms the family but also can be the starting point of *fitna* (trial, chaos) in society.

Why Do We Need To Work On Our Self-Esteem?

It may not be the easiest thing to treat yourself with self-respect when you may not have been nurtured, protected or elevated in the past. However, self-esteem can be relearnt to the point that everyone can, insha'Allah, enjoy high esteem, no matter what their past or their starting point.

Working on developing yourself is not easy. It requires courage, conviction, certainty, consistency and moreover it demands focus. This is the time to face realities and dig deeper; to look beyond the superficial, visible and tangible problems. When you look inside yourself for the first time, it is a scary place filled with feelings that make you uncomfortable, that make you cry and shake with fear. You may feel vulnerable – more vulnerable than you have ever felt before. This is the point at which the growth happens. Accept that you were never the object, never the victim and never the helpless. You are in charge, but only when you take the lead. Only when you decide to make the move, feel total ownership and be the conqueror of your own world, life, heart and mind, will you allow yourself to transform, change, develop, grow and break the vicious cycle of negative parenting. That only leads to unwell little adults that end up as the oppressor or the victim in a very intimate and 'restrictive' marital relationship.

It is time to identify underlying causes and aim to work on these, pull ourselves out, help our spouses out to remove themselves from and break out of the shackles. Pain doesn't leave us. Our parents' traumas are planted in us, and our own childhood traumas are directly shaping how we live and lead our marriage and family life. We relive the memories, right now, right here. It becomes the present. It becomes the marriage right now. We become our parent now to our child. Sometimes we may not know or realise what we are and what we have become until we look inside.

When we are strong inside ourselves, we are liberated from feeling betrayed, lied to or being made to feel guilty or even hopeless. We develop tools to manage and set boundaries, to be compassionate while protecting ourselves and learn how not to get on someone else's emotional rollercoaster who may need professional help.

Looking inside your self forces you to confront how you feel and why. Perhaps you find yourself in a black hole and trapped; perhaps you feel strangled, suffocated and drowning in the sea of marriage that never had a honeymoon period. You may have accumulating anger, severe lack of confidence that you are releasing in the form of abuse, violence, neglect, irritable behaviour and feeling disconnected. The following are signs that your self-esteem is low.

- Do you feel hatred, perhaps even self-hatred?
- Do you feel uncomfortable in your own skin?
- Are you overwhelmed by all that you have to do?
- Are you tired of trying to please everyone?
- Do you yearn for appreciation, acknowledgment, and a drop of love?

Self-esteem is like the foundation of your house. It defines the boundaries and the house will only remain upstanding as long as the foundations are strong. If this isn't strong then the whole house comes falling down. Similarly, your self-esteem is the foundation of you, your understanding and value and strength.

I sometimes ask some of my clients to take my pen from my hand. When I am holding on tight to my pen, then the ladies struggle to do this. That is me holding onto my self-belief, my values and my worth. If I hold on to these tightly then no one can take these away from me. If my pen is loosely held in my hand then the ladies have no problem in snatching it away, which is a reflection of how easily my worth can be taken and how easily another can have control of me.

You are enough because Allah created you enough. He gave you the means to live a life that is enough. **Allahu kafi** – He is enough for you and you become complete, sufficient and distant from that emotional emptiness. Allah loves you more than anything else. So even when no one else seems to care, your nearest and dearest seem to hurt you, then know that Allah is closer to you than your jugular vein and He is the Most Merciful. He has planned each detail of your life so that you can grow into your best self. This is the exquisite level of care and concern He has for us.

Although the terms **self-esteem** and **self-confidence** are often used interchangeably when referring to how someone feels about themselves, they are actually different concepts and it is worth understanding the difference when we are looking to improve our overall sense of self.

Self-esteem refers to how you feel about yourself overall; how much esteem, positive regard or self-love you have. Self-esteem develops from experiences and situations that have shaped how you view yourself today. Self-confidence is what you feel about your capabilities and skills. So if you are a good cook then you will feel confident in the kitchen, for example. You may still have low self-esteem because you generally feel that you are not good enough, but cooking is an area that you feel confident about. By focusing on the things you are confident in, you can change the negative self-talk and improve your self-esteem in general.

Taking the Control and Power Back

Self-esteem take two guises in married couples. Either they are in control or they are being controlled. We can give power and control to other people to use and abuse us. Low self-esteem is like a plant, which sways from side to side in whichever direction the wind blows. It can bend the plant completely and sometimes, even in bending, it will feel like it hasn't bent enough.

Different people will come into our lives and if we bend to please them all, we will never stand up straight. We will never have our own values, beliefs and self-respect that form our backbone and so we lose respect in our own selves. If we have no respect for ourselves, then no one else will. If we do not like ourselves, love ourselves or hold ourselves with importance, then no one else will and we only have ourselves to hold accountable for that. Our well-being does not come from the acceptance of others. Contentment and healthy self-esteem lie in the acceptance of oneself.

I talk a lot about people pleasing and there is nothing inherently wrong with that. But when we fixate on that to fill a void in ourselves, when we only do something so we can be accepted by another person, we may become disengaged with ourselves. It is then hard to separate whether it is we that is important or the other person. When the other person gets the message that you don't think highly of yourself, this gives them a chance to treat you in whatever way they wish.

One of the most common and easiest ways in which someone can chip away at your self-esteem is through thoughtless, offensive and rude comments about aspects of you such your weight or manner of dressing. A healthy self-esteem will enable you to reject their senseless comments politely and firmly. For those that cross boundaries, healthy self-esteem is able to say,

"That is enough" or "You need to learn to respect me and I'm not going to take any more criticism." This is one of the many steps and parts of the healing process. Having said that, it is very important to differentiate between feedback and criticism as well as our own responses to these.

Offering and receiving constructive feedback is part of personal development and requires growth and stability to be able to deal with. One of the greatest signs of self-growth is that you can discern which feedback to react to and take on board and which feedback is detrimental for well-being. There is no need for other people's opinion to guide you if it is not helpful, and negative thoughtless criticism does not have to become your reality.

Suddenly all the people that were used to putting you down will be challenged. They will, of course, continue, to do so for a while – the process of everyone else adjusting and accepting may take some time, but alhamdulillah if you remain true to your self, then you will slowly see that people begin to view you, speak to you, speak about you and treat you in a different way; that is, respectfully. When you set up polite and graceful boundaries, the dynamics of your relationships will change.

This is how you learn to take the power back. This is addressing the root cause of the problem. You may need coaching to help you through this but the first step is to know that it is never alright to take hurtful comments. We do not need to get aggressive or angry or rude. We do, however, state the truth with words such as, "I am sorry you feel this way", or "I feel that was an inappropriate comment."

The accepted norm in some cultures is that people should not answer back especially to their elders and this is to be respected. However, by stopping negativity in its tracks, you are actually empowering the relationship and adding boundaries that help the relationship to be more sustainable, healthy and nourishing for all parties.

Often when we receive verbal abuse and we are unable to set healthy boundaries, we may resort to more passive aggressive means of responding. This is not healthy as we harbour disrespect for others, so it is better that we are honest and transparent in our relationships and work to protect our self-esteem. Think back to the pen in your hand. You wouldn't let someone snatch that away for no reason. So it is worth holding on to your values and beliefs with the same strength.

Through self development work, people come to recognise how many years they have been abused without realising it. They become very angry at their perpetrator, or the individual they bent over backwards to please, as well as being frustrated and angry with themselves for having allowed this to happen. This anger needs to be channelled out gradually and counselling can give you the tools to help you protect yourself from self-blame, punishment and resentment.

This work all takes time. There is no illness for which Allah has not created a cure, so we must believe that things will get better with time and effort. I see clients come for one or two sessions and then stop. There is not much that can be achieved in that time frame and this is a process that takes time. Each journey requires its own length. However, opening a wound and then not cleaning it can make the wound more vulnerable and susceptible to infections, diseases and other problems. Sometimes that's even worse than leaving it unhealed in the first place.

Why is Self-Esteem Crucial?

If you have self-esteem, then you respect yourself and when you respect yourself, you give out a message to others that they have to respect you too. You will know that it is more important and healthier to live up to what you want to do, meaning your expectation, than to live up to others and what they expect of you. Self-esteem means that you don't have to prove yourself to anyone else, as long as you are sure of who you are and of your own goals. You will be happier knowing who you are and being more honest, authentic and genuine with yourself.

If you have poor boundaries, you leave the door open for people to make comments and judge you. These are internalised, consolidate your negative self-talk and negative beliefs about yourself. Once you own these negative beliefs and they become part of you, this has a direct effect on what you achieve in life.

We all have a personality we show to the world, the one that is for everybody, the one I call the public sector persona. Then we have another persona we show to those at home, and often our 'better' persona tends to be reserved for the public. Finally, there is the persona we have with ourself, the one when we are alone. This is our true self. How you see yourself has an effect on how everybody else sees you. Out of these personas, the most important one is who you are with yourself. If you have good self-esteem then you will have the confidence to be yourself in all circumstances and so these personas will not be so different. That is the point when you are comfortable being your true authentic self.

Having good self-esteem is not like having a magic potion which makes everything okay, but it will guarantee, insha'Allah, that you will be able to deal with trials or traumas that come your way in a stronger and healthier fashion. You will have the confidence to move forward and continue with your life, building your relationship with yourself and having a closer connection with Allah. A strong person is part of a strong Ummah.

Self-esteem does not stop you making mistakes or having learning experiences, but it does provide a strong safety net that will help you bounce back. When you fall, you will rise again because you have the confidence in your self. This is what self-esteem will offer you.

How to Raise Self-Esteem

To raise your self-esteem, you need to be aware of your thoughts and self-talk. When you recognise that these are negative or unhelpful, then you have to change the narrative. Recognise that you have choices and that you do not have to feel the way you do. You do not have to talk to yourself in the way that you do. You can change. The things we believe about ourselves become a self-fulfilling prophecy and only we can change that.

You can begin to believe in your abilities. You may start in thinking that you can't do something or achieve anything, but you have to sit and think about what is unique and creative about you, as Allah has created us with gifts and all of us has a gift.

Children have a positive and growth mindset. They are not afraid of a negative outcome and will try again. Otherwise how would children ever learn to walk, if they sat down the first time they fell over! So the key is in shifting our mindset from a negative one to positive one; from a fixed mentality to a growth mentality, and this is done by working on our inner beliefs. Essentially we are retraining the brain to help us be our best self.

Next Steps

- **Reflect.** It is very important to have time and space to think. Nothing changes unless we stop and think about where we are and work out where we would like to go, who we want to be, what we want to do. Part of this is accepting that you may have low self-esteem.
- Start by **writing what you are good at**, your talents and attributes. However unimportant it seems to you, write it down. It can be maths, poetry or making someone feel important or really beautiful handwriting. This may be something you can't think of all in one sitting but you can do over time. Add to the list when someone compliments you about something or you feel you have done something well.
- Then **set some personal goals** for yourself that you will work towards and measurably attain within a set time frame. It may be that you choose to commit a portion of the Qur'an to memory or that you would like to take a formal qualification in accounting as a starting point to setting up a small home business or you would like to run a marathon or go back to university. I am humbled by the change in the people who come to me from the timid people they once were to the high achieving, confident, productive successes that they have become. It is truly and tangibly transformational in the very way they are and speak, in their relationships and as parents and to society at large.
- Writing a **gratitude diary** can be very empowering. It is truly amazing to think about all that we have to be grateful for from Allah. This is such a powerful tool

against negativity and can reset the balance we have in our minds about all that is wrong with us.

- Keep a diary of words of wisdom, **motivating quotes**, lessons that you have learnt that day or week, inspiring stories that you have heard.
- Develop a **deep trust in Allah's love** and mercy and continuous support for you. This is profoundly healing.

This all helps in reinforcing positive beliefs and adding to high self-esteem. People find they are uplifted, calmer within themselves and in their relationships when there is positivity in their life. The things that hold us back may be fear, worries and hopelessness. By introducing this positive mindset and especially in writing, we can overcome these to attain the healthiest and most beneficial form of self-esteem and this aids us in becoming a better servant of Allah as well.

In parallel:

- **Avoid making comparisons with others.** It is important to recognise that not everybody can do everything. There are certain things that you are able to do and others you can't and this applies to the people you may look at and compete with. This is part of being human. Everybody has been uniquely gifted to be advanced in one method of learning and communication but not in another. This diversity and the unique and special way in which we have been created is a source for us to increase our gratitude to our Lord.
- **Explore and challenge limiting core self-beliefs.** The limiting and restrictive thoughts and self-beliefs you may be having now weren't part of you when you were born, so clearly something has happened along the way. It can be helpful to identify the causes of your current

set of beliefs and then to hold them up to the light. See how they can be challenged and guided to being more positive. In this situation, it is worth remembering that there is never failure – there is feedback. When we think that we have failed, there is a sense of being stuck, but when we take things as feedback, it feels like there is a way forward.

- **Du'a.** Allah gives us the power and divine support to change our mindset from being negative to being positive and if we are serious about this, then this should form part of our sincere du'a.
- **Leave the fixed mindset.** Negative core beliefs that have been picked up from the past can be limiting. They can make us feel that things have to be the way they are and there is nothing we can do about it; that we must accept and be patient (i.e. silent and inactive). Firstly, this is not in line with tawakkul, which requires the believer to strive with determination and combine it with good thoughts about Allah and reliance upon him. Secondly, while the human mind is wired, there is plasticity (the ability for the brain to change) that allows you to relearn and embrace different concepts in various ways. It is a great injustice to the beautiful creation of Allah to assume that all is done and nothing can be changed. We are created to become better, improve, develop and always increase our good deeds. Had we been created a certain way and been expected to live our lives in that way, then Allah would not have created the tools of forgiveness, repentance and good deeds. In our religion, Allah emphasises the significance of effort and determination and that starts with a growth mindset.

> ***And whoever fears Allah (and keeps his duty to him), He will make a way out for him (from every difficulty). And he will provide him from (sources) he never could imagine...*** (Surah at-Talaq 65:2-3)

When we make an effort, Allah responds. Even the call of the believer to Allah is an effort, a determination, a form of striving that is beloved to Him. Yunus ﵇ called to Allah:

> ***He called out in the pitch darkness: 'There is no god but You! Glory be to You! Truly I have been of the wrongdoers.'*** (Surah al-Anbiya 21:87)

> ***We responded to him and rescued him from his grief. That is how we rescue the believers.*** (Surah al-Anbiya 21:88)

This is how Allah inspired and commanded the whale to spit out and throw Yunus ﵇ out onto a safe area. Yet, this rescue came following the cry and du'a and increased worship of Allah by Yunus ﵇. These verses teach us the etiquettes of asking for help from Allah: reflection, acknowledgement of wrongdoings and shortcomings, seeking forgiveness, strong determination and belief. This is what initiates rescue from Allah and improvement of the situation, insha'Allah.

I invite us all to embark on a journey of reflection and exploration, of tawakkul and growth so that we can, insha'Allah, strive for excellence through healing.

Chapter 5

Breaking the Cycle

This chapter will address those key areas that we can all work on to improve family life for ourselves right now as well as for the future. On an individual level, this means that family life looks more like the Qur'anic prescription of love and mercy and the members of the family can each fulfil their individual potential. Done collectively, this will have a huge impact on the community, our strength, our unity, our achievements and productivity within the wider setting. The chapter is divided up as follows:

- Positive Patience
- Secrets of a Successful Marriage
- Communication
- Proactive Parenting

Positive Patience No Matter What!

All the trials that we go through are ultimately from Allah regardless of whether the scientific cause is determined to be genetic or environmental, psychological or financial:

> ***We will test you with a certain amount of fear and hunger and loss of wealth and life and fruits. But give good news to the steadfast.*** (Surah al-Baqarah 2:155)

It is important to learn what 'positive patience' is and to adopt the Qur'anic patience that Allah tells us He loves. This is patience that draws us closer to Him, increases us in tranquillity and insight. This is patience that removes doubt, fear and hopelessness yet gives us the pain that is part of the healing process itself. We are assured that:

> ***No misfortune occurs except by Allah's permission.***
> ***Whoever believes in Allah - He will guide his heart.***
> ***Allah has knowledge of all things.***
> (Surah at-Taghabun 64:11)

Thus our first response should not be blame or regret, it should serve to strengthen our belief in Allah because that is what will guide the heart. A good response is:

> ***Those who, when disaster strikes them, say,***
> ***'We belong to Allah and to Him we will return.'***
> (Surah al-Baqarah 2:156)

Having turned to Allah, the next part of positive patience is change. It is for us to reflect why Allah chose this test for us and how He wishes us to respond to it. Patience is not the stagnant, static quality that we sometimes mistake it to be where we wait for the trial to finish without a response to it. It is a dynamic state that praises Allah, that seeks to understand why this trial has come to us and what outcome Allah is trying to teach us by it, and then to strive towards that outcome.

Secrets to a Successful Marriage

Much of this basic foundation has been covered in the first book in this series, **Secrets to Successful Marriage**. However, I think it is important to briefly touch upon some of these aspects again due to their important and fundamental nature as factors that heavily impact a marriage. However, I would recommend reading through the book for details and case studies.

Love and Affection

It is the duty of a man to look after his wife: to provide, ensure she is healthy, safe, happy, flourishing in her worldly affairs as well as her deen. In addition to this, women need love and affection. The Prophet ﷺ has demonstrated through his example that this may be achieved through joking, sharing, teaching, hugging, sleeping on their laps, feeding them and most importantly forgiving and maintaining gentleness and kindness even when they make mistakes.

Respect

Given the weight of a man's responsibilities, Allah has given him a greater need for respect and more of a say and authority over decisions to ease these responsibilities. That is not to say that women do not also need respect. They also want to be treated respectfully, listened to and valued. Often when we think of respect, we think of talking in a respectful manner during a discussion, argument or behaving respectably. However, respect can be a bit more multidimensional especially for men.

Men derive their satisfaction and sense of self-worth at home from being involved in decisions, happenings and steps, being listened to and acknowledged and praised for their views, opinions and thoughts. They like to be kept in the loop, as it were, and know that their ideas and contributions are important.

Respect is the first thing that exists in the hearts of a couple, it comes and nests itself in the deepest blood vessels and feeds and allows the growth of love. When people part and separate, the first thing that leaves is respect and then eventually it is the love that fades away.

Trust

Trust in a marriage can be broken due to a variety of factors including: inconsistencies occurring, a broken promise, a controversial text, a stolen glance, secrecy around money matters, and so on.

This can have an impact on the relationship for many years because no solution has been sought through communication. It is very hard to bring back those feelings of security once trust has been broken. Insecurities then cast a dark shadow over the relationship. The negative situations keep coming back into every argument because the feelings of hurt have never been resolved. It is, therefore, imperative to nurture trust once broken, by reassuring, reaffirming and exercising honesty.

Transparency is essential. The mindset of both people should be that husband and wife are on the same team and any actions have to reinforce that. One of the beauties of marriage is to have that openness where you can say anything to each other and know everything about each other and know that it is all held in a safe, non-judgemental space. These are very important things to bear in mind when it comes to trust. Building that trust, keeping that trust and holding on to it forever are key principles in a successful marriage.

Roles and Responsibilities

Look after your obligations and you will automatically get your rights.

Sometimes we focus so much on looking at our own rights and wants, we forget the importance of fulfilling the rights others have upon us and completing what Allah has asked us to do. The starting point should never be what someone should be doing for you. This is an egotistical viewpoint and is not helpful in the long term. Firstly, **you** need to concentrate on what **you** need to give to the marriage, and do it in the best possible way. If you do that, insha'Allah, you will get your rights and needs met. I am not saying you should just give endlessly when your spouse doesn't give back. This advice applies to both husband and wife, who do their duty and surrender to Allah's will, knowing that their reward lies with Him.

The woman is the primary care taker at home and is mainly responsible for raising the children. Typically, the man is earning, taking care of matters financially and making sure the family is protected. In essence, we know these roles can be interchangeable depending on a family's needs and circumstances and most importantly mutual agreement.

The lesson is that we have to stop and reflect upon is this: if one person is completing a role and is doing the best they can in the situation, they are doing what Allah has asked them to do. So if she is holding the fort at home, even if it's difficult, her reward is with Allah. If he is having to work long hours to earn money, this is where his reward is. So if we see that our spouse is doing their best, we can be more appreciative and grateful in our response to them rather than criticising that we had too much to do and our wants have not been met. These issues can be brought up gently and a mutual solution sought later, but the mindset is one of appreciating our spouse as a first response.

Emotional Intelligence

The simplest definition of emotional intelligence is that it is the ability to recognise, understand and manage one's own emotions and then recognise, manage and influence others' emotions. It is more than just the recognition of emotions or the validation of feelings or empathy. It starts from within yourself. High emotional intelligence is typically self awareness, self management and self recognition and acceptance. This means the individual is deeply connected to their roots and inner dimensions, and is in tune with their body and soul.

Improving and increasing our emotional intelligence will mean that we are able to be authentic, genuine and in sync with our emotions, likes and dislikes and are able to display this with positive outlook and clarity whilst recognising, understanding, influencing and catering for the emotions and emotional needs of our spouses. These are the miraculous ingredients of any successful relationship and particularly a blossoming marriage.

I have been mentioning various tools and techniques throughout the book, that can be utilised when communicating with our children, spouses and even how to be with ourselves. The deeper aim of these suggestions and techniques is to increase emotional intelligence.

The field is too vast to cover in this book, but I invite my readers to explore the concept of emotional intelligence further and aim to improve your own skills, to instil this in your children, spouses, home and all other relationships. Some of the common guidelines to raising children with high emotional intelligence are: to validate and label their emotions, listen and pay attention to minute changes and expressions of emotion, encourage them to recognise and identify their state of heart, mind and soul as well as others', sharing emotions and dealing with their discomfort.

The Here and Now

In times of instability, be that in life or in marriage, we forget that life is not always about the here and now. We cannot envisage how our decisions in this moment are going to affect our life in the future. For those couples who find themselves in a cycle of conflict, think about when you were a child/teenager. What wacky idea did you have about the future? Think about your dreams, aims, goals, and how you thought you could change the world. Looking back you were so sure of yourself then, but you can see now the unrealistic aspects of your desires and your own immaturity.

Now look at you as an adult thinking about separating. Are your thoughts, expectations and beliefs realistic, mature, thought out? Do you really think the grass is greener on the other side or will you just be switching out one set of problems for another? Where do you see yourself as a couple in ten years time? Sometimes with age comes wisdom. Each part of your life demands a different version of you. How you live up to and adapt to that version is dependent on your needs of not only today but also tomorrow.

These questions are used to create a projection of the future. The here and now of marital discord causes emotions of frustration and anger. In that moment, the only solution we tend to see is to end the marriage. The first solution to marital discord is resolution. Divorce should always be the last option as it is not the only way forward. The first step is always to get counselling. This will allow you to gain impartial advice and the suitable tools and environment to rationally consider every aspect of your decision. The reason why I emphasise going to counselling is because many people regret getting a divorce especially when children are involved. Only after every avenue of resolution has been utilised, should one seek a divorce as it is the decree of Allah.

I realise many husbands find it very difficult to come for marriage counselling due to the stigma surrounding it. Marriage counselling has helped numerous people to resolve their issues, stay in their marriages and live a peaceful life. A healthy marriage is a harmonious and conducive environment for yourself, your children and their future. It is also the bedrock of our society. Having a strong family is important for society as a whole. We should focus on resolving and getting help and set aside the stigmas surrounding the things that are beneficial for us.

Communication

If I had to pinpoint one issue that brings couples to me, it is the breakdown of communication between husband and wife. When everyday issues, which may recur over the years or be rooted in past conflict, are not dealt with, this causes the couple to feel angry and betrayed and leads to a breakdown of trust. When both parties are wary and distrustful of each other, they cease to communicate effectively. Effective communication is the starting point to resolving any issues, in this context, marital issues.

Communication can be divided into three parts:[7]

1. Words make up 7% of communication
2. Tone of voice makes up 38% of communication
3. Body language makes up 55% of effective communication.

When we are having face to face communication, we need

7 The Mehrabian Rule (named for Albert Mehrabian who was best known for his publications on relative importance of verbal and nonverbal communication).

to remember these three elements and the power they have in conveying our message.

Although we don't think about it, listening is also a really important part of communication. According to Surah 2:187, we are garments for one another, in other words, warmth, protection, mercy, provision and elevation for each other. Listening skills can be utilised in a delicate way so that we live by this ayah every time we listen and cater for each others' needs. Listening, understanding, valuing, acknowledging, hearing and walking with our spouse, along the same path, with complementary thoughts and ideas is an invaluable gift that cannot be replaced or substituted with anything else. No gift, physical contact, gesture or treat is equivalent to this powerful and mind-blowing gift.

If you don't listen, understand and address the needs and wants of your spouse, it can lead to resentment, grudges, hurt, upset and grave misunderstandings. It is very important for me to reiterate this – we have to take care of each other's needs in marriage. We cannot dismiss them or not give them validation.

Many times this is the root of the problems in a marriage. Husbands complain in a general way that she is argumentative or controlling. Wives may say he doesn't talk to me or listen to what I am actually saying. These are just statements that walk around the actual issue. Verbalising the actual problem is harder than it sounds. Behind the argumentative nature or the avoidant personality will be someone who is hurt because they are not praised, accepted, listened to, made an effort for and that is difficult to express without being vulnerable. So the message may be, "I need attention" but it is covered up in the form of aggression, anger, frustration, withdrawal, turning away and distraction. This is the same for women and men.

At this point, the layers need to be peeled away and each others' actual needs and wants identified. This requires each spouse to ACTIVELY listen to their other half – to actually focus on what the other person is telling you. That means taking in information, digesting it, trying to understand it, and then trying to evoke the feelings that are appropriate to that conversation. Once that happens then the healing of the marriage can begin.

Active listening involves the body, mind, soul and brain collaborating to be receptive to all that the speaker is giving you. This may be a tone of voice, word, intonation, gesture, mimic, body language or perhaps just a move. There's a poem that is often taught or shared as part of coaching or counselling programs:

Please Listen

When I ask you to listen to me
and you start giving me advice,
you have not done what I asked.

When I ask you to listen to me
and you begin to tell me why
I shouldn't feel that way,
you are trampling on my feelings.

When I ask you to listen to me
and you feel you have to do something
to solve my problem,
you have failed me,
strange as that may seem.

Listen! All I ask is that you listen.
Don't talk or do – just hear me.

Advice is cheap; 20 cents will get
you both Dear Abby and Billy Graham
in the same newspaper.

And I can do for myself; I am not helpless.
Maybe discouraged and faltering,
but not helpless.

When you do something for me that I can
and need to do for myself,
you contribute to my fear and inadequacy.

But when you accept as a simple fact
that I feel what I feel,
no matter how irrational,
then I can stop trying to convince
you and get about this business
of understanding what's behind
this irrational feeling.

And when that's clear, the answers are
obvious and I don't need advice.
Irrational feelings make sense when
we understand what's behind them.

Perhaps that's why prayer works, sometimes,
for some people – because God is mute,
and he doesn't give advice or try to fix things.
God just listens and lets you work
it out for yourself.

So please listen, and just hear me.
And if you want to talk, wait a minute
for your turn – and I will listen to you.

Anonymous

What you can do:

Active listening incorporates the following ideas:

- **Repeating** the conversation, content and information through your own or their words – this is called paraphrasing.
- **Do not introduce your own reactions** or well-intended comments and impose your own ideas and opinions onto the speaker.
- **Let the speaker take the lead in conversation.** This may mean that you remain silent for a long while and perhaps only aid the continuity with minimal encouragers such as 'yes', 'ah', 'ok'.
- If you do not understand the comment or statement, then **ask for clarification.** This will help you not to assume and allow you to walk the same path with the speaker.
- **Reflect back** on some of the conversation to show that you have understood. Reflective statements and questions can aid empathic connection.
- **Support their feelings,** for example, "I see you're feeling quite helpless right now."
- **Allow the speaker to correct you,** guide and lead you and take you on their own journey. Let them choose what they would like to focus on and filter out of all of the things that were shared.
- **Effective questioning** is a tool that I feel should be made compulsory in schools. Your questioning style should elevate the dignity, respect and self-esteem of the speaker and not be interrogative or even demeaning. The point of effective questioning is to facilitate the speaker to digest, process, rethink and reflect. It is about helping them to unpeel the layers of

some aspect of what has made them angry and upset. It is not to feed your own curiosity or to make someone feel bad. When you are in active listening mode, it is important to prioritise the person you are listening to and focus on what they have selected to talk about.

Conflict Resolution through Communication

Arguments or discussions should not take place to compete with one another, to insult one another or to release anger and frustration. It is to reach a resolution as to the points of difference. The couple needs to sit down with the mindset of trying to work things out, recognise what they are doing wrong, wanting to make the situation better, being open about the root cause of the problem with honesty.

Knowing and learning more about the past influences on our spouses, in particular their relationships with their parents, will equip us with the knowledge, tools and skills to facilitate a healthy, effective and beneficial communication. Often couples are quick to complain about each others' behaviours and actions but do not reflect and contemplate on the reason and causes of this pattern of behaviour.

If he gets unresponsive then it may be because her communication style is aggressive and critical. If that is similar to what he grew up with, then over time, he will have developed a hard protective shell and adopted a coping mechanism that blocks this type of approach out and starts to ignore this type of communication. In this case, she would be well advised to change her approach and method of communication: her tone, choice of words and ways of putting sentences together. Requesting that a need is fulfilled gently will yield better results than shouting it. This example can be applied to many other requests, demands, needs and wants:

"Yunus, is it possible for you to find some time this weekend to put up the peeling wallpaper in the kitchen? We need to repair it and I would really appreciate if you could do this."

There is a very specific request here with a time frame, delivered in a calm, non accusatory tone of voice. Many spouses are surprised to see that this actually works.

Case Study: Comfort Zone

Emotional Turbulence: Nargis says that she is finding it difficult to communicate with her husband. He doesn't actually listen and he doesn't really talk. She says that she may be discussing a certain matter and will try to engage him in the conversation. However, he will just nod his head and not reply. When she asks him to do any household task he will say, "You do it. I can't do it." It's as though he doesn't want to test the boundaries, and just stay in his comfort zone.

His Background: Growing up Jahangir had experienced extreme forms of stress and anxiety as his parents had been highly critical and made him feel a failure. This had affected his self-esteem and he was very scared of failure.

Solution: I asked Nargis to always reassure him and try to build his self belief. The language I asked her to use is, "I really believe in you. You can achieve ..." The key was to use positive words around him and to reassure him that if things did go wrong that he could always try again.

It took her some time but the end result was that Jahangir came out of his comfort zone, and began to try doing DIY, organising family trips and so on. Once Nargis began to believe in Jahangir, he began to believe in himself.

Knowledge of the past and upbringing of your spouse will aid you in tailoring your approach and communication to them to get the best results and facilitate effective communication. If you identify parenting styles and experiences in childhood and upbringing and formulate a communication method based on that, you will see change very quickly. A spouse that has been bullied as a child will have grown up believing that they are not capable of doing or achieving anything. For them, it will be productive to have a spouse that encourages, motivates, boosts their self-esteem, gives them a little leeway for any mistakes and shortcomings, and helps remove their fear of failure. A spouse that hasn't been offered love, affection or physical closeness as a child will benefit from gentle speech, softness, calm and affectionate manners. This is the way to get the best out of them. Remember that husband and wife are on the same team and should be supportive and appreciative of each other.

Many couples think that it is not their problem to fix the issues of the past in their spouse. To them I would say, you also came with baggage into the marriage and you would like for someone to be understanding and patient with you. If you are patient in helping your spouse get through their issues, you will be rewarded with the same, and your partnership will be strong and loving. Isn't that what we all want? That does require some effort. We can often be very empathetic and concerned to help out with other people's issues. Perhaps it would help us the most to start in our own homes.

In addition to support, appreciation is very important in marriage, and if you want to get the most out of your partner, appreciate the smallest things they do. It doesn't matter whether the job your spouse needs to do is part of their wider role or duty.

That is not the point. You still need to acknowledge and show appreciation and ensure you provide positive reinforcement instead of teaching and preaching a sense of entitlement. If you apply this formula, I guarantee you, you will receive more in your relationship, because if people appreciate you, you will incline to do more for them. This is human nature.

We can refer to our spouse with a term of endearment or a pet name. This will soften the heart. Simply speaking in a loving way can also go a long way to keeping the home atmosphere pleasant. It does not always come naturally and we may have to smile and force ourselves to be extra sweet sometimes. This is worth it. We would do it for our boss to keep our job, for example, so how much more important is it to do it for our spouse? If it keeps the marriage alive, if it keeps conflict to a minimum, then surely it is worth it. Marriage is the bedrock of society and if that is strong then the community will be strong. If our home environment is pleasant then the children we are bringing up in that environment will be more balanced. Everything has a ripple effect; it is not just about what we want or feel in the moment.

Having said that, it is still important to be open and honest with each other about your feelings in a kind way. If you are feeling something, say it and the thought behind it. So, for example:

Ali comes home from a hard day at work and his wife doesn't ask him how his day was and doesn't ask if he would like a cup of tea, as she usually does.

Scenario 1: Ali is upset and doesn't talk to Huma throughout dinner or help do the dishes after dinner. Huma shouts at Ali for never doing anything and they spend the whole evening not talking to each other.

Scenario 2: Ali tells Huma as they sit down for dinner, "When I came home and you didn't even ask me for a cup of tea, I felt very upset." Huma explained, "I am sorry, that was not deliberate. I have a migraine today and only just managed to get dinner ready." Ali appreciates that Huma got dinner ready for him even though she was ill and clears away the dishes after dinner.

When you want to tell your spouse how you feel, using "I" statements is more powerful than, "You made me feel..." Huma offers an apology and an explanation and shows Ali that she was not being neglectful of him. He, in turn, understands and help her out.

In scenario 1, he did not communicate his feelings and she never had the opportunity to explain herself. His feeling disrespected and neglected would have grown and festered over weeks and weeks ending up with the belief that she doesn't care. All that it takes is simple and timely communication to prevent.

The Prophet ﷺ asked us to make seventy excuses for our brother and yet we live in a time where we struggle to make just one for our spouse. Making excuses, forgiving and communicating feelings without accusation should be a habit. It should be a habit to ask each other how the other is feeling, if everything is okay, if there is anything they would like help with. This will prevent grudges, resentment and prolonged upset feelings.

An ingredient of making excuses is empathy. If we can't walk in the shoes of our spouse, how can we make excuses for them? Empathy can only be built once there is knowledge and understanding of your spouse's world, their past, their internal frame of references and experiences. When you communicate in an empathetic way with your spouse you are more likely to have their affection, concern, and for them to attend to your needs as well.

This requires us to be open when we need something. Spouses cannot mind read and give us what we want or need without us asking. If you need a hug, ask. Then appreciate it when it is given. This is positive reinforcement. Tell him you cooked his favourite meal for him instead of waiting for him to work it out and then feeling resentful if he doesn't say anything. All of us need training and help to become more skilled in loving and reciprocating.

How to Argue Respectfully

In cases of conflict, it goes without saying that it is highly recommended for both parties to maintain control over ourselves and especially our tongues. When we end up losing our good manners and common sense, we may overstep boundaries, make irreplaceable and irreversible mistakes and hurt each other in ways that are difficult to heal and improve again.

Swearing, shouting, and throwing things at each other has become the norm as part of a heated argument in a marriage. We need to first remember that before we are a wife or husband, we are a servant of Allah and are accountable for our abuse, neglect and misbehaviour. Even if we are upset, angry or hurt, our marital relationship is one of the means by which Allah tests us and it facilitates our path to attaining Jannah.

If we are too emotional, it is worth removing ourself from the room and taking a break and picking up the discussion when we are both calmer. This is constructive and we are stopping ourself from degenerating into toxic behaviour. When things get heated:

- Fear Allah at all times
- Remember your manners at all times
- Look for resolutions when you are calmer
- Most importantly desire a good and positive outcome, rather than needing to be right or having the last word.

Choosing the Right Time to Talk to Your Spouse

Timing is everything. It is not just about how to speak to your spouse but when. Over the years, you will know and begin to understand when your spouse is more focused, when they are in a good mood, and so on. These are essential when it comes to a sound marriage. Some people are more relaxed after a meal, others in the morning, still others in the evening. This is about being aware of what would be appropriate so that communication is beneficial.

If he is always tired after work and she is telling him her troubles as soon as he walks through the door, then that may not be the best time. If she is concentrating on cooking, then it may not be the best time for him to ask her for a favour. This is intuitive.

It sounds obvious but communication is easier when both part-ies are actually focused on each other, facing each, with eye contact. This may mean waiting until the children are asleep. It certainly means removing yourself from your phone, tablet, TV or laptop and giving each other your full attention. There should be actual time set aside to talk (not just in the car on the way to the in-laws) and not just about the admin side of the household but to actually talk about planning, reflecting and contemplating on life, the hereafter, personal or professional development together, setting goals and evaluating progress. Taking the time out to think of what both of you want and how you can be on the same page is a healthy step forward. Ensuring you have a good time to communicate will help both of you master the art of communication. Some couples are only together to do the shopping, meet family, and drop the children somewhere. This is not a great forum for effective communication. Once couples have mastered the art of communication and made time for it no matter how busy the schedule, then other little niggles will usually fizzle out.

Most marital tension is due to spouses not knowing what the other wants or how they feel. I can't reiterate enough that spouses are a team that both need to work together. Trying to work separately will pull away and separate the family unit. If she is in the driving seat and he is in the passenger seat and she is trying to accelerate and he puts the handbrake on – well, no one is going anywhere! The roles and responsibilities and aims are not fulfilled. Someone has to drive and someone has to take the passenger seat. Nothing says you cannot swap at any time.

Communication should be about everything – from the mundane daily life issues to decision making to future plans, even if they are in their infancy. If you have a new business idea, then tell her. If there are changes in your work place, then tell him. Be supportive and excited or concerned for your spouse. Hiding the fact that you have lost your bonus for this year can create mistrust and lead to complexities in the relationship. The norm should be that spouses are in tune with each others' lives, have empathy and a good understanding of how the other may feel and what may be going through their minds. If you know she is having trouble at work, then you will be less demanding about issues at home while that is happening. If you know he is wanting to start a new business and save some money, you can hold back from buying that gadget this month.

People think that it is only women who need romance, affection, love and marital connective care. In fact both spouses have a 'love tank' and it is filled through different means and ways for men or women or across different individuals. That is one of the joys of marriage – in exploring the languages of love that suit you both.

Without a language of love – be it verbal affirmation, physical connection and contact, gifts, quality time or joyful intimacy –

there will be frustration, resentment, upset feelings and in many cases trigger a search for these things outside the marriage. Often this is attributed to men only, but this is actually an issue of both men and women. We, as humans, are created to keep our tanks full and have a deep yearning for our relationships to be fulfilling, nurturing and secure. If those essential nutrients do not come from our spouse, then this leaves the door open for others to provide those ingredients and that corrupts hearts, ruins marriages, family units and most importantly the hereafter.

Providing the essential nutrients – the building blocks of love and affection – not only nourishes the spouse, it heals and protects the marriage, the family and the hereafter of the couple which is why there is great reward in every act in the marital relationship that nurtures and instils love and mercy. Spending, sharing, laughing, consulting, even intimacy, are all acts that are rewarded by Allah because they are essential to the foundation of a strong Ummah.

Couples will say they don't have time for these things or they are too busy with many other things, that things have changed for them since they had children. From the life of the Prophet ﷺ, we learn how every moment can be utilised to nourish relationships. Love and mercy is hidden in the subtle, genuine and continuous acts and words between spouses. Loving is not in expensive dinners or foreign holidays. Loving is in the ease and simplicity of daily life. It is worth reading and studying the seerah from the angle of the Art of Loving. In fact, studying the seerah together can soften hearts and facilitate stronger bonding between spouses. This can tell us of love, mercy, justice, compromise, sacrifice, suffering, grief, victory and loss if we choose to understand and take on board the lessons offered to us by the best of human beings, so that we may elevate ourselves.

Case Study: Buried Love

Emotional Turbulence: Shahana and Hussain have been married for two years; often these are the most difficult years. Although they loved and cared for each other in the early months, the marriage soon became difficult and was a source of distress. They struggled to meet the needs of the in-laws and balance out visiting times. Both felt the other wasn't supportive enough in visiting the other's parents, and commitments and visiting times and frequencies weren't fair. Shahana felt her mother-in-law was interfering in the relationship and always ringing her son to check up on what they were doing and what was happening in his household. At the end of the two years, Shahana and Hussain fell apart and had tired each other out and felt resentment and frustration towards each other.

Solution: In counselling, I asked them at the end of the discussion, "How do you feel about each other, if we removed all of the in-law issues and all of the other problems that seem to cloud the marriage, what are your true feelings about each other?" Hussain said, "My wife means the world to me!" and Shahana said, "I really love my husband." But when they first came into the session their body language was tense, they had a lot of resentment and hurt towards one another.

Often when communication breaks down, couples end up angry and frustrated with one another and they forget that they still have these other key emotions for the other person such as love. Negative emotions cloud our thoughts and feelings, and dictate the words that we use during arguments. We need to connect back to those organic and original feelings and help each other to express and maintain those whilst validating the other more negative ones.

Proactive Parenting

Nurture the root to bear the fruit.

Although this is a marriage book, there is a deep connection between upbringing, marital life and parenting. No book on marriage is complete without looking back at upbringing and neither is it complete if it fails to look forward at parenting. One must dive and explore the roots in order to reap the fruit.

Just as we have explored the traumas of the past that have given rise to the baggage we hold today, which is hindering us to have our best married lives, it is vital to link the effect of this on our children. Otherwise the cycle continues. We struggle our whole lives to keep it together and deal with the fallout of various traumas only for our children to do the same. No community can thrive like this.

What you can do:

We, as parents, cannot live in abusive environments, create an illusory bubble around us and make believe that our children don't know. Yet surprisingly that is what my clients think when I ask them to consider the impact on their children. In reality, children are like sponges, they absorb everything, not only spoken and seen, but also tensions in the air, and feelings in the heart. We need to be brave, face reality and learn to offer change and healing for our children alongside preventative strategies.

If we could squeeze that sponge (our children), we would see drip out every single negativity and ill-behaviour that we have given to them in their surrounding. Here are a few steps to take that may aid the process of helping and supporting children in negative environments:

- **Be Brave:** We cannot pretend our children don't know. As adults, we need to ensure we take responsibility and ownership of the situation and recognise that they hear, see and experience everything. Even babies will know that something is not quite right. They will be unsettled, unhappy and perhaps display behaviour that reflects the 'mood' of the family. Traumatic events and constant battles at home can cause anxiety in children. This may not be a clinical manifestation to begin with and perhaps even be very temporary. However, it can manifest as constant stress and depression in the later years of childhood. In other words, we need to be brave and face up to the reality of how our children are affected now and how this will affect them in their adult lives.
- **Be Honest:** We must be honest with our children and demonstrate and provide a sense of reality to them. We need to speak to them, without pain, sadness or criticising our partner about the facts of the situation. It is vital to have an age appropriate and open conversation with our children, to encourage and facilitate a healthy discussion about the struggle that you are going through. When children don't have background or context and they hear fighting or see abuse, they have no framework for what is happening and so it is internalised as anxiety and severely impacts self-esteem. If you can have a conversation, explain what is happening, ask how they feel, give them the space to be heard then they have an outlet. It is beneficial to do the following:

- ✓ Active listening
- ✓ Attend to their feelings and emotions
- ✓ Validate their emotions and experiences
- ✓ Respect and protect their dignity
- ✓ Be apologetic about things that they may see and hear that can be quite disturbing
- ✓ Don't shy away from hearing their feelings, facilitate the discussion and exchange of emotions and demonstration of their feelings
- ✓ Give them plenty of time and safe space to connect to you
- ✓ Make them feel prioritised and safe
- ✓ Include them and instil hope and trust
- ✓ Make du'a together and remind them of Allah. This brings light upon light into their hearts. Crying, asking and calling upon Allah, instils great hope and grants them a stable personality as they learn at a very young age to trust and rely on Him and know that He is greater and above everything else that may come their way.

Again I will emphasise that this should be age appropriate. Any discussion should be delivered in a very sensitive careful way, being mindful of the amount of information and depth shared, bearing in mind the child's capability and receptivity and most importantly nature and age. Over sharing and exaggeratedly open discussions can be harmful to children, too.

The point about being open is not to offload your feelings on your children, but to bring them out into the open and put them in a framework. This will help children reach a clarity and comfort with their feelings, instead of isolating and shutting down because they cannot handle what is going on, or worse, think that it is their fault.

- **Look out for symptoms:** You know your child, and if you see signs or symptoms that are out of the ordinary, make sure you attend to them by getting the appropriate help. Keep an eye on your child and be alert and attentive to the reaction you see in them to 'events' at home, bearing in mind that some children react and absorb quicker than others.
- **Avoid arguing in front of children:** This is something all married couple should strive for as it makes all the difference in the home environment for a child. However, it goes beyond just not arguing. We should be aware of our tone of voice, looks, body posture and language which may all reveal anger, frustration, fear, sadness or resentment. These are even easier for children to notice, so we need to ensure that we do not argue and fight with our words, eyes, body language and mood. This is a very difficult task and perhaps the spouse may not agree and sometimes even do the very opposite. This is the ideal that we are working towards and whatever effort we can make in this regard is always better than none. Allah will reward us for our intention, effort and constant prayers to Him.
- **Don't use them as pawns:** We need to avoid using our children as messengers and as part of an ongoing argument with our spouse. This means not saying, "Go and tell your mum this...", "Go and tell your dad if he ever tries and..." You might think that this is neutral but it is actually using the children, making them part

of the argument, and exposing them to toxic content. There may be no shouting involved but the children have become the messengers of ill feeling very early on in their lives. This is not only inappropriate, but very difficult, heavy and unbearable for children. The reason why some children of battling adults walk around tired and lethargic and sad is because they are literally carrying the weight of their parents' issues and it is too much for them. We really have to be attentive to our children's wishes, desires and worries.

- **Running away is not always the solution:** Once all avenues have been exhausted, many people do decide to part ways, but this is more complex and hurtful if there are children involved. I always counsel that every option should be considered and tried before making irreversible decisions like 'escape'. The disclaimer is that if you are in a marriage that is verbally, emotionally, physically, sexually abusive, and is a threat to you or the children, if and when there is harm, this is a serious crime and requires professional and immediate help. Sometimes in our community we normalise pain and harm and think that being inactive in the face of oppression is patience. It is not. However, when there is space for development, improvement and willingness on the part of both spouses to make some adjustments, I recommend putting every effort into repairing family life. There is no illness that doesn't have a cure. This is what we have to rely on and trust in Allah that He will aid us in every trial. A couple may benefit from external intervention in the form of speaking and receiving help from helpful, wise and supportive family and friends; speaking to health professionals; or going for counselling (individual, marriage or family).

- **Help your children with their emotions:** Your children may feel ownership and a sense of guilt for what is happening at home. Let them know and support them in their understanding of the situation and remove the pain, shame and guilt from them by explaining what is happening in a way that they can understand. Reassurance, explanation and emotional connection helps them to grasp the situation better and feel convinced that nobody is upset with them. We have been given the message that men should not display their softer emotions or share their feelings. This is causing untold dissatisfaction and problems in marriages. We have to raise our boys (and girls) as expressive individuals that are rich in emotional vocabulary. This will help them to become more courageous, conscious, and empathetic.
- **Recognise trigger points in your spouse:** Act upon the stimulus that you see and feel. Once you recognise something is happening that may trigger an episode or an outburst very soon, you may want to avoid that confrontation and ensure your children are in another room, in the garden, perhaps at a neighbour's or may be handed over to a friend to play outside. This can be quite difficult but developing strategies to better handle and control the effects of such episodes can be helpful. This is very useful for children as well, because they can see that even when their parents are not getting along, they are the priority and their safety and comfort is taken care of. Someone has taken the effort

to make sure they are not in the cross-fire. This can instil solace, warmth and trust and offset some of the effects of what is happening.

Protecting Children from Abuse

This is one of the most traumatic experiences that can happen to a child and has happened to a few of my clients when they were younger.

Case Study: Shame

Emotional Turbulence: Razia is 26 years old with three children. She has a loving and supportive husband, but feels no connection, no desire, and no wish for anything. "I feel worthless and completely useless. If my husband wasn't taking me out," she said, "I would stay home and not do anything for weeks." We explored her low mood, lack of interest and feelings of abandonment, loneliness and low self worth.

Her Background: She was sexually abused by her own uncle, who would look under her dress. She also had a sexually abusive experience with an outwardly religious figure in the community and he had exposed his private parts when she was very young. She developed guilt, feelings of blame and self-hatred. She was unable to tell anyone and although she became withdrawn, she says that no-one noticed.

I present this case study so that we may learn to pay attention to subtle changes that happen and appear in our children. Children do not know how to act out trauma and distress but they display behavioural changes. In the case that children feel they cannot come out and speak, then we, as adults, need to be aware of what those changes can be. Children may start hitting their siblings, becoming very withdrawn and very quiet, sometimes very abusive, loud and attention seeking.

We also need to reflect on whether our child finds us approachable as a parent. Would they be able to confide in us about anything and know that they would get a compassionate response? If parents recognise any symptoms that are outside of normal behaviour for that child, the first question they need to ask is, "Is everything alright? Is there something you would like to tell me? It seems you are very angry these days." This validates their feelings, and you are opening the doors for them to share and find security.

It is also important to know whom we leave our children with and where they are. A number of perpetrators of child abuse are known to the child and so we should be careful at all times. Do not have blind trust that your child is safe everywhere and with people unless they are well-known to you. To this end, it is wise to keep interactions within Islamic boundaries, avoiding people of the opposite gender no matter what capacity they are in, unless they are mahram. I must insert the caveat that I have heard of rare cases where same gender abuse has taken place and abuse has occurred at the hands of close family members. As parents, we can take the precaution of being aware, setting and teaching boundaries among family members and ensuring that open dialogue is always available to our children. We can also teach them what the boundaries of decent conversation and words are, what is appropriate physical contact and what is inappropriate.

Ask children how they feel with certain interactions, about certain people and if they have ever felt uncomfortable. These questions will bridge the communication gap and ensure your children will open up to you. We should not neglect and delay this education and ensure from the age of three, our children develop a sense of secure and healthy physical interaction and develop a personality that is confident to express discomfort and dislikes that may be indicative of abuse.

When children don't talk and come across as 'weird' due to their lack of social interaction, other children who are a little bit more dominant can make the vulnerable child the target of their abuse and bullying. Children block out things, perhaps they are vague in their communication, but we still have to make the effort to connect with them.

It is essential that we work on ourselves to heal and develop and learn to cope with our scars and at the same time make the utmost effort to try and equip our children with the correct trust-based relationship with us, their parents. We should be the role models for good insight into what is acceptable and what is not acceptable for them and teach them boundaries.

We can do our best and we then leave things in the hands of Allah while maintaining a deep trust in Him.

Next Steps

- **Bonding:** Establish healthy, sound and very good relationships with your children. We all need to aim and work for bonds in which our children feel safe and welcomed to open up, discuss and feel settled. We need to offer unconditional positive regard which includes an approach that is non-judgemental. Some of the things that stop children from confiding in their parents are:
  - ✓ Lack of attention and ability to practise active listening
  - ✓ Being judged
  - ✓ Blame, shame and being accused
  - ✓ Fear of being ignored, neglected, punished
  - ✓ Fear of the perpetrator and their threats.
- **Effective Communication** is essential. This allows us to remain in the loop, be well-informed and be in tune with our children's worlds. Effective communication is based on three things:
  - ✓ Giving them time, not just any scraps of time but designated and high quality time
  - ✓ Making them a priority and putting them first
  - ✓ Unconditional love. This entails that children are always loved, not based or dependent on their success, following instructions or 'being an obedient' child. The love needs to be there and shown regardless of their performance, slip ups and nature.
- **Be Observant and Analytical** of your child's emotional, physical, social, psychological and spiritual state. When something traumatic happens to a child, their thinking, behaviour and emotional world will change and this

will show. We have to be cautious, alert and keep our children's state under the microscope.

- **Teach and Empower Your Child** with age appropriate knowledge about respect and boundaries, about what is acceptable in behaviour and speech and what is not. They need to know about their bodies and what is appropriate in which context, and this needs to come from us, not school or friends. We need to validate and confirm the sense of security and protection our children innately have about their bodies. The fitra is to clothe, to cover, to protect and to be modest. So many influences around us are working against this fitra. Giving our children the right to say no, express dislike and be in ownership of their body, clothing and dignity will help them to recognise and vocalise threats, uncomfortable experiences or even disturbing looks before traumatic events take place.

Chapter 6

There is Hope in Healing

Healing the Inner Child

When traumatic events happen in childhood, we have to pay attention to that child in the past, and let him or her heal and deal with the hurt and scars. When you reach into the past, you will be communicating with the 'broken child' inside. This is the trapped child within the adult body, with all the traumas and constraints of the past, preventing you from reaching your full potential as an adult. It is part of the healing process to go back and walk side by side with that inner child. You may find yourself crying or self soothing like a child. Part of the healing process is about pulling out that child and letting them express and release, letting them know that they are safe, secure and protected with empathy and unconditional positive regard.

Caring for and healing that inner child requires effort with an intention to heal for ourselves, for our marriage and for our children, so that collectively, as a community, we have a stronger base. Marriage and parenting are bedrocks of society and we must get these right, if we care about our hereafter and about the unity of our Ummah.

I would reiterate that in dealing with the past, we love our parents, we are dutiful, we are respectful, BUT this does not justify the effects and causes in our well-being at the moment and that of our children. We need to reflect and approach the situation with compassion for ourselves and for our parents.

We have looked at a variety of problems in childhood and the emotional turbulence that this can give rise to in adulthood. We have, by the mercy of Allah, explored some solutions and shared reminders. In this chapter, I would like to wrap up by looking at some ways in which we can move forward in our healing journey.

As Ibn Al-Qayyim mentions, the bird has two wings of which one is hope and the other is fear. We have discussed the many issues, problems and worries that may cause fear. However, whenever there is a trial, Allah promises ease, comfort and light at the end and even during the trial. There is always hope, and we must always begin our healing journey with that in mind.

Many people wonder how long it will take to heal. This is not only difficult to answer because it is a very personal journey, it is especially difficult because everybody's needs, wants, sensitivities are very different. However, like anything else in life, success in healing lies in 'organic growth'. That means allowing the surroundings, time, nutrients, experiences and reflections to be natural, innate, genuine and authentic. This will require plenty of time as it is a non-linear process and that we cannot push along according to our schedule. The less rushed, hasty and impatient you are, the more effective, meaningful and deep-rooted the healing will be. It is a step-by-step process and requires full attention, full dedication and strong trust, reliance and the best of expectations of Allah.

This is also a process that requires real commitment and consistency, whether that is through therapy or self work. The significance of this particular matter is severely overlooked and trivialised. Think of a wound that has been opened up, left uncleaned and fully exposed. While there are some things you can do to expedite the healing, the healing will take place at a pace set by your own body. If you simply open the wound and then leave it uncleaned, you cannot heal. This is a process that you need to see through to the end but the rewards that you will reap are even greater. It is never easy to open up the past and look inside yourself, to be vulnerable, to go into your dark areas, but it is highly rewarding and absolutely necessary for our mental health. It is through the access into the deeper inner world, digging out the hidden and untangling the knots, that we can reclaim our hearts and minds and lives now and for the future. If we were in a similar position of pain and 'dis-ease' physically, we would not hesitate to seek help. We must learn to do the same for our mental health.

The main concerns that people have surrounding seeking counselling are: time and expense. If it was a matter of physical health, many people would find a way to prioritise it. There are a number of more cost effective and free options. As to time, we make the time for whatever we feel is important. We have to collectively rewire our understanding of priorities and urgencies. Our mental health and mental well-being and that of our whole family is very important.

Consider the 'car of life'. Your whole family is in this car, everyone who is important to you, but no one can drive. No one has passed their theory test or driving test or taken any lessons. If no one knows how to drive, sooner or later, at best the family will get lost, and at worst, there will be a car crash. We are losing the way, and we are having car crashes that look like acrimonious divorce, domestic violence, suicide, anxiety, anger, to name just a few.

Someone needs to take ownership and know how to drive, know where it is that the family is going and how to get there safely. This entails a sound mind with a vision and a thought process for what we want to get out of life and what we want for our children. That mind is the 'power house'. It needs time and attention. It requires a mental rewiring, emotional courage and great commitment to be consistent, determined and most importantly the decision to be captain of the ship. If your spouse is not on board, that's not a problem. If your children were drowning you would not wait for your spouse to rescue them, you would not think about whether you could swim or not, you would try to save them.

Next Steps

Here are some steps that, insha'Allah, will help along this vital journey:

Intentions

Wanting to heal and approaching healing with sincerity and commitment is crucial. Your intention has to be pure. It is helpful to set out in your mind what your end goal is otherwise it is too easy to drift off part way through. Then put your self into healing: with your words, thoughts, actions, time, effort – everything has to be aligned.

Goal

Our goal, the ultimate goal, is the pleasure of Allah. To see His countenance, for Him to be pleased with us and for us to enter into Jannah, our home of true happiness and contentment. The place in which all pain, trouble, grief and loss will end and be forever lifted. Blessings will be eternal and salaam will be spread and given at every opportunity. This is where the servant of Allah is blessed with that which their heart longs for most. Where there will be no bad feelings or animosity, no hatred or emotional baggage that makes our days and lives difficult. It is the place that will offer the best of servants the delight of tasting and seeing and breathing and living everything for the first time. In it there is what no eye has seen, no ear has heard, nor has it ever entered the mind of man. That life will have no end and no termination. The pleasant experiences, emotions and feelings and pleasures will be eternal and there will be no sense of boredom.

The teachings of Islam point us to **ihsan** – the beautiful, the highest, the most excellent. This hadith of the Prophet ﷺ encourages us to be determined and focused on the best and most beautiful of places,

> *"If you ask of Allah, then ask Him for Al-Firdaus, for it is the middle of Paradise and the highest part of Paradise, and above it is the Throne of the Most Gracious."* (Bukhari)

Reflecting on the blessings and gifts in Jannah, it is easy to see why we desire these states in this world. But part of life is that these perfect states of emotional balance are not ours to reach here. It is only for us to try and achieve the states that Allah describes for us in the Qur'an in so many places: *taqwa* (Allah consciousness), patience, gratitude, humility and so on. Only then, insha'Allah, can we hope that it will be said to us:

'Enter them in peace, in complete security!' We will strip away any rancour in their hearts – brothers, resting on couches face-to-face. They will not be affected by any tiredness there and they will never be made to leave. (Surah al-Hijr 15:45-47)

Although we may be mentally fatigued and exhausted from the trauma, struggles and our battles, we have to pull ourselves up. We have to fight and challenge our nafs and not submit to its desires and wishes. When we win over our nafs and allow it to be shaped by our remembrance and the teachings of Islam, it will become less of a burden and a hardship on ourselves. One of the best ways to overcome this fight and battle is to make du'a.

Du'a

This is the weapon of the believer. We have not been created except to worship and call on our Lord. There are two types of du'a: reactive and proactive. The reactive du'a is when we pray to Allah in response to a specific trial that has befallen us. For example, Yunus عليه السلام called out to Allah when he was in the belly of the fish. Then there are those where we request a future state – either protection from Hellfire or for pious children or wisdom – before trials strike us. For example, Ibrahim عليه السلام prayed for right judgement and Jannah (Surah 26:83-85). These are proactive du'as. Ibrahim عليه السلام made many of these and it is worth having a look at his du'as as they focus on a future state and he is asking his Lord to help realise his vision. It is important that we have a future state in our minds for ourselves, our families, our Ummah. It is important that we articulate that in our du'a as a means to draw closer to Allah and simultaneously exert all our efforts to achieve that state as far as we are humanly able while leaving the rest to Allah. Du'a alone is not as effective as du'a with effort. Allah helps those who help themselves.

Do not underestimate the changes that can occur when you combine du'a and effort, especially when things seem difficult and impossible. Allah out of his mercy, grace and generosity never returns a request that is asked or put together by a slave of His. He is Al-Kareem. He will always be and remain Generous. I have witnessed real life stories that are the very reflection of the Names of Allah. It only remains for us to turn to Him in sincere du'a.

Acceptance

No healing can come about unless there is acceptance that there is a problem, in one's self and within the marriage. Escaping, running away or a defence mechanism that is based on avoidance will not resolve the issues. We have to look in the mirror and be honest about our shortcomings and realities. We may not like what we see but that is a mercy. It is precisely because we do not like what we see or what we have become that we are forced to change for the better. We are social beings that influence every one around us and one of the most important relationships we have is the one with ourselves.

It is important to acknowledge our pain as it defines our relationship with many other people in our social environment as well as our bond with our Lord. If we bottle up that pain, deny it, refuse it, then it will simply eat away at us to the detriment of our psyche (and eventually physical health) and those around us in the ways that we have looked at in Chapter 2. We sit in denial because we think that it will protect us. In fact, acceptance and validation are the shields that will protect us from harms and emotional dangers. It is okay to say, "It hurts" or "I need help", or embrace the fact that, "I am struggling to cope!" It is okay to cry and not know what to do immediately but at least that is the start of the healing journey. Denial might make life less messy right now but causes untold damage to the inner child in the long term. That damage looks like increasing anxiety levels, anger, negative thoughts or even a breakdown. We do not have to allow things to escalate to this level before we decide to make a move and take charge of our well-being. When we accept the things that are part of us, that belong to our self, this is not only healing, it is rather empowering and enriching to our personalities and development.

Repelling Negativity

The fastest way to sink our own ship is to live in a bubble of pessimism and negative thoughts and think, "Why me?" Positive thinking will change our perspective on the situation, which in turn will govern how we think and behave. For example, if you drop something, your first thought may be, "I am so stupid and clumsy. I can't do anything right" and we play that in our head throughout the day. We need to start saying, "I dropped something. I will clean it up and the issue can stop there. It happens to everyone." When we change our self limiting comments and thoughts, that is the first step to treating ourselves with respect.

Another aspect of this is to focus on what you do have as opposed to what you don't. We have looked at the benefits of keeping a gratitude diary in Chapter 4. This doesn't mean that we ignore our issues. They still need to be dealt with in order not to cause harm. The point of this exercise is to be able to convert our negative energy into positive energy that does not just sit and ruminate, but is optimistic enough to create change. To see beyond the daily incidents and arguments and be able to place them as part of Allah's plan for us. The path to healing is based on the ability to see reality and say, "Alhamdulillah, this was good for me. Because it taught me patience and gratitude. Because it forced me to make these changes. Because it made me struggle and grow." This reminds me of the story of Imam Abu Hanifa:

> Imam Abu Hanifa was not only a great scholar but he was a successful merchant as well. Once while he was teaching, some people came to him and told him that all his ships (containing all his goods) had sunk. So Imam Abu Hanifa paused for a moment while teaching, then he calmly said, "Alhamdulillah" and continued teaching. A little while later the same people come back to inform him that they made a mistake and his ships were all fine. So again he paused for a moment, said, "Alhamdulillah" and continued teaching.
>
> His students questioned him about his response. He explained that when he was first told that his ships had sunk, he paused to examine his heart and when he found it unmoved, he replied, "Alhamdulillah." Then the second time when he was informed it wasn't his ships, he paused again to examine his heart and again found it unmoved, so he replied, "Alhamdulillah." He was thanking Allah not because of the gain or the loss of his ships and worldly wealth but his "Alhamdulillah" was about the fact that his heart was not attached to the gain or the loss.

Mindfulness

One of the most powerful ways to retrain the brain is mindfulness. When you enter a state of mindful awareness, you bring your tension to the present moment and you observe each thought, feeling and sensation as it flows through your consciousness. You live and breathe in the moment; recognising, absorbing sounds, voices, colours, sensations. This is a good way to come out of the so-called 'robotic state' that we find ourselves in. Close your eyes and try this. Try and feel beyond the normal sensations and perceptions. It is very relaxing and healing to the body and the mind. This is similar to stopping and pausing the clocks. Allowing time and space to be still and prolonging the seconds that we usually overlook and never enjoy. In that reflective state, we can ask ourselves what we are feeling and thinking. Those thoughts that we normally brush away because we are too busy will thank you for allowing them to be heard.

> *When we are mindful, deeply in touch with the present moment, our understanding of what is going on deepens, and we begin to be filled with acceptance, joy, peace and love.* (Thich Nhat Hanh)

This is something that we can try to use to increase our focus in salah.

Self-Care

Self-care is not about being selfish but being self aware enough to know what you need to be your best self. I don't mean spa days or having a bar of chocolate while watching TV. Real self-care requires you to put your life under a microscope and really highlight and work towards your aims, objectives, and interest areas and have dreams and desires of your own. Your self-worth and sense of purpose depend on this. Everyone has their own way of feeling good, contented, being in a state of gratitude, having a state of good iman. The quality of your self-care and working towards keeping your heart, mind and soul in the best place is part of your gratitude to Allah for creating you.

It is not possible to be a people pleaser, be neglectful of yourself and sacrifice your self-worth at the expense of other people and then stand in front of Allah with the positive, hopeful and visionary mindset of a true believer. Having lofty aspirations accompanied by du'a and solid aims to work towards allows us to keep going through the tough times and gives us a sense of purpose in the more comfortable times.

In marriage, it is very important for both parties to have their own interests, their own worlds, their own ambitions. Husbands and wives learn, grow and develop as individuals and they also set better examples for their children. Successful and happier marriages, in my experience, are those in which couples are excited, stimulated and striving in their own way without neglecting each other and their responsibilities.

Look Happy

There is some wisdom in faking it till you make it. Trying to smile, dropping your shoulders and holding your head up even when you don't feel like it increases your positivity and is healing to you and others. A hadith says smiling is charity. We need that charity for ourselves first and foremost.

Unconscious Living

This describes the state we are in most of the time. We are always on the go with too many things to do. Children slot in somewhere. Spouses may get neglected in the heap of things to do. Tick box mentality is what we are suffering from and it is about getting things done and finishing the day with a list of ticked items. That, for us, is a day of achievement. The problem with this unconscious way of life is that what suffers is our relationships with ourselves, children, parents, in-laws, spouse and most importantly our relationship with Allah. When did salah or spending quality time with our children get reduced to a five minute tick-box listed item? When did life get reduced to: wake up, clean house, drop children, work, pay bills, collect children, eat and sleep. That leaves no time to talk or share or enjoy or care or worship. We are disengaged from the people and the nature around us. We have forgotten how to discuss plans, thoughts, dreams, faith and go for restoring walks in nature. Let us at least make an effort to get some of that back.

Make a Priority List

One of the ways to conscious living is to make a list of priorities. Family life is like a garden that constantly needs cleaning, tidy and attending to so that it will flourish, grow and give you a restful place of beauty. That tranquil space doesn't maintain itself. Very soon it overgrows and becomes an eyesore that we avoid. It is so important to have a sound family environment in which the family is together – an environment of openness, love and faith. Once you have made a list of priorities and impactful actions, then see it through. That means letting go of doing things the way you have been, but that just means that you will get different result from what you have got before, which is exactly what we want. Consider the wants and needs of yourself and the whole family. If the whole family pitches in for 15 minutes, this leaves 45 minutes of whole family time, rather than one person cleaning the kitchen for an hour.

Communication

Although I have written a whole section on this topic in the previous chapter, I would like to touch on a few points in this chapter. When the needs of everyone are reasonably accommodated, then family life can be harmonious. How do we know the needs of others if we do not ask? How would we expect others to know our needs if we don't talk about them? It really is that simple. Marriages tend to fall back to assumptions and mind-reading which only leads to frustration and misunderstanding. A little talking and little listening goes a long way. This forms the rhythm of communication.

When someone tells you what they are feeling, especially children, it is vital to validate their emotions, thoughts and experiences. Allow them to say what they are feeling without judgement or opinion, so they feel they can be who they are in that space.

Communication is just as much about what is said as well as what isn't and when. The space and time that fills the gaps between talking needs to be respected. Some people need more time and space to reflect, settle down, cool down and get back to us whenever they feel settled, comfortable and secure to do so. The greatest gift you can give to your family is undivided attention at a time when it is needed and requested, and equally the quiet moments when those are needed. All of these collection of behaviours build up an emotionally intelligent household and an environment which fosters love, affection and self actualisation.

Forgiveness and Letting Go

As we go through life, people will say things that hurt us, experiences will challenge us and circumstances will try us. Only Allah knows the wisdom and reasoning behind these exposures that we witness. It is not for us to understand everything and our ignorance is a mercy from Allah that protects us.

There comes a time in life when we can either choose to hold on to everything and let it burden us. Or decide to progress, move forward, forgive and let go of various things. This is a very specific and unique journey to each person. There is no particular set way or time to do this nor is there a pattern. In my experience, a starting point may be to reflect on why others may have been, thought, acted or lived like this. How does it feel to be in their shoes? It can initiate empathy, connection and some sense of understanding. That doesn't make bad actions right nor make a justice out of an injustice. It relieves the burden for us, the sufferer, and alleviates some of the pain.

The healing process can be facilitated through writing a letter to the 'source' of the pain. This is useful for those who find it hard to move on, forgive or even accept. For those who keep repeating the past in their heads, it may be useful to get it out on paper. Sometimes the difficulty stems from the 'source' no longer being alive. It may be that it was the parents that are the cause or part of the cause of the struggling and perhaps they have passed away. These letters can be sent, kept, read out in a therapy session or destroyed. Regardless of the choice, this can be a liberating process of freeing the heart. Here is an example of a Letter to the Source:

My Dear Mother,

I pray and hope that you are well. I felt I had to write this letter to let you know how you made me feel growing up. You don't know that I am, at the moment, receiving counselling which has made me realise who I am today. I've never felt good enough, I was never happy, I couldn't stand up for myself, I always felt anxious and depressed yet never understood why. Now it's become so clear to me, it was never my issue, it was yours. I remember so many times growing up when you would go red in the face and walk off, frustrated and angry at me if I did anything a normal child would do. You constantly blamed me for everything that was wrong in your life.

Growing up I realised it was better to be alone than in your company. You were never emotionally there for me. Coming back from school, you never asked how my day was. I remember when I was 5, I looked at you, you looked so sad, so unhappy, I always thought it was my fault.

My counselling has made me realise that perhaps you were as depressed as I was. And perhaps your past was a shadow that affected you just as my past has affected me. But just to let you know, today I am in a much better place, I believe I am good enough, I didn't realise how many skills and talents Allah has given me. I have let go of the past, and steadily I am moving forward. I am going to be going back to university this year. I am going to complete my degree, and I have become somebody that I am happy with. I no longer blame myself.

For a long time I felt very angry at you, that is why I didn't ring when you would constantly ask me now I am an adult.

I carried so much anger and hatred for you, for what was denied to me as a child – love, affection and many things more that a child needs to become a competent adult.

However, I have now come to terms, as my counsellor explained, that you can only give what you have and perhaps in your past you had some traumatic events that made you the person you are today. So I forgive you, and I pray that you find some peace, just as I have done.

Your loving daughter,

It is a daunting, painful and scarring experience to accept and embrace the experiences and pain. It is frightening to uncover the layers and see what we find. It is terrifying to confront the swirl of emotions that come up with this de-layering. Once the sources, roots and reasons have been identified, it can be devastatingly difficult to ever imagine being able to forgive or let go or even convey that fact to someone. They don't have to know. Forgiveness is for you. It is the balm you put on your wound to soothe it. It does not absolve the other person of wrong doing. Once you forgive, you will find the baggage you were holding onto no longer weighs you down. You can breathe deeper and smile brighter. The acidity of hatred and disgust and injustice don't eat away at you anymore and your heart is now free to grow positive things in. When you forgive, you open the door to seeking forgiveness from others and from Allah, as the Prophet ﷺ used to do a minimum of seventy times a day. It may help to dissociate from people and cling onto Allah, in recognition of the fact that only He will not wrong or oppress. He is the only One that can save, protect and heal.

Within the broader idea of forgiveness, is **self forgiveness.** We sometimes punish ourselves for our choices and decisions in life. We play the blame game, which drains us of our positive energy. But we need all our energy for productive change. All that time spent in blaming ourselves can be better used in setting goals for a better future, insha'Allah. All of our experiences, good and bad, make us who we are today. To want to erase 'the bad bits' means to deny the lessons learnt, the strength gained and the clarity found. It means to deny that Allah's mercy wishes us to grow with all our experiences.

Focusing on the Present

Many people live in the past, get stuck and struggle to move on and live in the present. It is important to learn to separate the past from the present. The past is inextricably linked to the present. Childhood traumas lend their colour to present daily life, interactions and perceptions. They pull you into the past and convince you that there is no difference between that and the present.

Allah by His mercy gave us the ability to forget, to live from one salah to the next and to adopt healthier coping mechanisms. When we choose to stay stuck in the past (and it is a choice of ours) there is no way to change, develop, grow and improve. This does not imply that the past should not be dealt with. It absolutely needs to be. However, hiding behind the back of 'the past' and justifying today in that light is very damaging and unhelpful for healing.

Tadabbur al-Qur'an (Reflecting on the Qur'an)

We have a most powerful tool at our disposal that we often don't make use of in the best way. The answers are all in the Qur'an: the healing, the peace of the heart, the descriptions of the hereafter, Creation, the stories of the great people who suffered, how they connected with Allah, their emotional journeys and ultimate victories. It is all in there if we reflect:

> ***Mankind, admonition has come to you from our Lord and also healing for what is in the breasts and guidance and mercy for the believers.***
> (Surah Yunus 10:57)

Dealing with Destructive Thoughts

Changing your thoughts to impact your behaviour is part of healing. Everyone goes through various forms of thoughts and some of them are more intense than others. Sometimes these can even overpower the brain and body to the extent that we might feel like we are going to explode. So it is worth knowing what to do in these times of extreme pressure. These are typical Cognitive Behavioural Therapy (CBT) techniques: if you can change the thought, then you change the feelings and thus you can change the behaviour about the trigger. This helps in reducing the pressure build up.

Another means of reducing the destruction of thoughts is to question them directly. Which of my thoughts are based in evidence and fact? Which of them are preconceived notions and assumptions?

Thoughts that are repetitive can be equally destructive. They prevent you from sleeping or thinking because your mind is too full and overwhelmed by disturbing views, worries and opinions. Taking them out of your mind, and writing them out, will help empty and relax your mind. Whilst writing them down you may get some insight, patterns and formulating solutions and clarity in your sight and vision with respect to the next steps.

To this end, it may be worth keeping a Worry Diary. Allow a few minutes a day to pour all your worries into this diary. This allows you to worry at a particular time and you have to consciously make the effort to avoid worrying about these things at random times. This can be quite difficult in the beginning but gets easier to do over time. This is a very powerful tool to shift attention and focus on a particular area and develop insight into what is worrying us. This can be coupled with a data log – a diary or log of your thoughts, highlighting the good bits of the day, the kindnesses and achievements. This is helpful to boost self-esteem and also override the negative and disturbing thoughts.

Finally, having hobbies and building up a supportive network are useful ways to relax the mind and reduce the pressure of thoughts. It lets the creative side of us come to the fore and relives the pressures of home.

***

Throughout this book, we have uncovered some causes and symptoms of emotional turbulence and angst in marriage and family life. We have looked at ways that past traumas can form our core beliefs and how they rear their ugly heads when we are adults. We have dug deep and looked, not to address the symptoms, but the root causes. We have looked at ways to repair ourselves from deep within by changing our mindset and working on self-esteem. This must be accompanied by du'a, salah, tawakkul, positive patience and reflection. Without the whole package, it is almost impossible to shake yourself out, renew and refresh yourself and embark on a journey to put all the valuable and precious pieces of your very own organismic and organic self together. Once we apply patience, special patience, positive patience, patience that entails deep desire to do work, struggle, sweat combined with trust in Allah, that He surely is the Most Kind and only wants good for you and that He will aid you on your path, you will attain that which will free you and allow you to live your best life.

May Allah grant us the healing of our breasts and minds, purify our intentions and actions, make us of those that, through their healing, become the best leaders of the pious and grant us the highest and best place near Him in Jannat al-Firdaus. Ameen.

And of His signs is the creation of the heavens and the earth and the diversity of your languages and your colours.

Indeed in that are signs for those of knowledge.

(Surah ar-Rum 30:21)